Assertive
HUMILITY

Emerging
from the ego trap

Assertive
HUMILITY

Emerging
from the ego trap

STUART TAYLOR

MONTEREY
PRESS

First Published in 2013
by Monterey Press
PO Box 319
Carlton North VIC 3054
Australia

www.montereypress.com

Author contact: stuart.taylor@assertivehumility.com
Website: www.assertivehumility.com

Cover artwork, design and typesetting by Scarab Blue Design

Author:	Taylor, Stuart, 1969- author.
Title:	Assertive humility: emerging from the ego trap / by Stuart Taylor.
ISBN:	9780987581303 (paperback)
Subjects:	Taylor, Stuart, 1969- Cancer--Patients--Australia--Biography. Humility.
Dewey Number:	616.9940092

Dedication

To the love of my life – my wife Peta.

The last decade has represented an unpredictable and enormous run of health and life challenges. These challenges continue. Prior to diagnosis, our life was always on full throttle. Lots of exciting location, employer and family changes for both of us. Throughout, an attitude of "of course we should go for it, the worst-case outcome is we go back to doing what we did before" persisted.
As it has happened, this courage to take risks and pursue a dream has never required a retreat back to base camp. It was this attitude that was a guiding light through the journey post-diagnosis. It was your strength, particularly over the last decade, that gave strength to me when I was at my most vulnerable and emerging. It was your strength that provided stability to our children.

In all of this, you have been the rock of strength, courage and optimism.

Acknowledgements

Beyond my Dedication to Peta, there are so many people to thank, both in supporting my post-cancer journey as well as with the writing of this book.

To my mother Dorothy, thank you for your strength, support, guidance and love. To my father Geoff, while you weren't here for the journey I have no doubt your example and strength of character was/is my guiding light. Enormous thanks to one of my spiritual guides, my sister Janine. You have provided an incredible platform of strength through our philosophical conversations, naturopathic support and by introducing me to The Gawler Foundation.
My brother Sean, thank you for your humour and guidance in encouraging me to become less of a nerd and more of a socially relatable human being. To my mother-in-law, Carol Sigley – wow! What a pillar of strength for Peta and I during this last decade, particularly in light of the premature loss of Peta's dad. Carol, thanks for your realistic optimism. Thanks also to Peta's sister Kim, who came to live with us to provide support.

To the many friends who were there to support Peta and I in all manner of ways during those challenging times. Mother's group stalwarts and RAAF brethren deserve an extra special mention.

To the people at Heinz who gave me enormous support beyond what could have been expected. Firstly, my dear friend Glenda Thomson. You were the first colleague with whom I shared my diagnosis. I will never forget your reaction and response. To then CEO Tracey Quinn, thank you for your huge empathy for Peta and I with support during radiotherapy and extended leave of absence during 2002.

To Ian and Ruth Gawler and other wonderful human beings at The Gawler Foundation helping hundreds of thousands of people deal with cancer. What can I say - you changed the course of my life!

To Dr Sven Hansen at The Resilience Institute - an inspiration for thousands of people. You gave me the pathway and education to move to a new future. I love the work we are privileged to do together. Thank you.

Thank you to my book writing support crew, David Brewster (Clarity in Words) and Tricia Mahoney (Scarab Blue Design). Talk about taking a proverbial pigs ear to create a silk purse. Thanks to my generous foreword writers and book reviewers: Dr Charlie Teo, Rebecca McGrath, Dr Sven Hansen, Dr Ian Gawler, Bob Santamaria and Dean Salter.

Finally, thanks to my children for enduring and thriving through the journey. Joshua (16), you are an incredible and savvy young man with such a strong voice for change in our world. Llewellyn (15), you are an inspiration of potential with a heart the size of an ox. Claire (13), my beautiful girl - your dedication to excellence and care for others is amazing. Lucas (6), a ball of hope - what a joy to see you grow and evolve in your new life.

Foreword by Dr Charlie Teo

At the time I received the final draft of Stuart's book, I had recently undertaken a global initiative with the Cure For Life Foundation in which we brought together brilliant minds from across the globe to look at how we might use different perspectives to solve the complex problem of brain cancer. During this workshop I experienced a life changing revelation – that some of the biggest blocks to finding a cure were in fact the attitudes and egos of people working within a system. Unfortunately, these individuals become negative forces that restrict other people and systems from flourishing.

Emerging from this workshop, attended by many of the world's most esteemed scientists, was a simple solution. We have to move from an 'ego' based system to an 'eco' based system, and to do that the system of science needs to shift from a hero model to a host model ... one that nurtures and supports researchers rather than one that encourages a silo mentality and fierce competition. In turn, the common good will prevail, and fast.

Being a black belt in karate, I grew up with the notions of stillness, mindfulness and clarity of thought and it is the discipline around these that has carried me forward during my career as a neurosurgeon. I learnt the art of listening, a sense of humility, a great appreciation for humanity and a love of people, devoid of any judgement which serves to separate one from others. I was bullied at school and am acutely aware of being marginalised, yet this experience shaped me in positive ways. It made me grateful and proud to be an Australian and drove me to demonstrate compassion towards my companions. I am known as a man who doesn't withhold truth, and as I ponder the concept of honesty, I am acutely aware of the impact truth may have on people. I have found that the most resilient and egoless are often those who embrace truth easiest.

We all have a desire to love and be loved, yet the hallmark of love is 'being'. This book guides the reader through this journey of allowing and being, craftily written so that it not only makes change seem possible but inspires the reader to pursue it. Stuart gives great strength to the reader and a forthright pathway for the evolution of individuals, communities, corporates and humanity as a whole, through the wisdom that he so graciously shares with us.

It is my hope that brain cancer no longer diminishes lives, for if it does the Stuart Taylors of this world, who have so much to contribute, will miss out on making their important contributions to humanity. Ultimately this would be humanity's great loss. I encourage those reading this book to support the work of the Cure For Life Foundation so that we can curb the rise in brain cancer and find answers to treat, manage and prevent the disease, sparing future generations of its burden.

Dr Charlie Teo, AM, is a neurosurgeon and a board member of the Cure For Life Foundation

Foreword by Rebecca McGrath

As a business person who regularly has a significant backlog of non-fiction books to read, I will often rely on personal connections and recommendations to prioritise my reading. In this context, I read Stuart Taylor's book with interest, enthusiasm and perhaps the same initial question many other readers will have: is the concept 'assertive humility' not a contradiction in terms? Upon completing this reflective, first person account by Stuart, my conclusion was quite to the contrary. In the development of his hypothesis, he proposes assertive humility as a higher level of consciousness that embraces purpose and presence as well as compassion and caring. Put more simply, as he describes it, it is "a more authentic way to be".

When I first met Stuart Taylor several years ago, I was living the busy and driven executive life that he too had experienced earlier in his career. My interactions with him through the Resilience Institute made me reflect (as do many who have attended his programs) on the way my work controlled and to a large extent defined my life. I was struck by Stuart's insightful and thoughtful delineation of the role that physical, psychological and spiritual resilience plays in our lives.

Through memorable interactions with great leaders of both people and thought during my career, I have become a true believer in the value of authentic leadership. Unfortunately, when we look around the Australian business community today, we see too many leaders who are confined and controlled by their egos or their focus on positional power and authority.

In *Assertive Humility*, Stuart Taylor unravels what is behind this lack of authenticity in so many of us. This is done engagingly through his use of personal refection as well as anecdotes and references to some of the world's great psychologists. He explores the importance of the awareness of spirit, through a focus on values and purpose; the power of positivity and optimism; the impacts of under-caring and detachment; and the effects of approval seeking and dependency.

Stuart's personal journey, including his near-death experience with brain cancer, provides the reader with a deeply emotional and at times witty account of how he enhanced his own level of consciousness on his journey towards assertive humility. His practical examples and daily practices differentiate this book from many of the 'self help' books available today. Indeed, Stuart's understanding of big business culture and the factors that drive and motivate individuals to succeed affirms the great value of the concepts and mental models which he proposes in *Assertive Humility*. This will have particular value to those who are interested in improving their own leadership and impact through an enhanced level of self-awareness.

Stuart's journey has led him to explore the much debated issue of work-life balance. Whilst he concludes there is no magic formula, he is a great advocate for the investment in and the maintenance of one's own energy, and asserts this to be a much more effective approach than achieving some arbitrary separation in time (i.e. between work and family time). Energy in Stuart's context goes well beyond mere physical fitness, including time for self-reflection, and any other activities that 'rejuvenate the soul'. For any business person who is struggling with fitting everything into their day, Stuart Taylor has some helpful and experienced advice.

Assertive Humility is, above all, an intensely personal account of transformation. Stuart shares with us his story from childhood, his life-changing experiences and his deeply considered reflections and advice for "a more authentic way to be". A search for purpose, presence, mindfulness and equanimity will take you a long way on Stuart Taylor's journey.

Rebecca McGrath is a non-executive director of CSR Limited, Goodman Group, Incitec Pivot Limited and OzMinerals Limited. She is a member of the Advisory Council – Australia – J.P.Morgan.

PROLOGUE

Waking up

Assertive Humility

You're living the dream.

You've got a great job. The hours are long – fourteen or more a day – but that doesn't matter because you're operating at the sharp end. Enormous intellectual challenge, working with powerful people, intimately involved in the big decisions. Work is fulfilling – totally fulfilling. It's stressful but it's also a constant buzz; adrenaline hit after adrenaline hit. You're spending money and you're earning money.

You're working amongst the elite – recognised as elite – and enjoying the benefits as a result. You're well looked after: travelling well, staying well, eating well. There's no denying that the platinum cards, five-star hotels and hatted restaurants are enjoyable, but in the end they are a reasonable reward for the effort you're putting in and the sacrifices you're making: the big decisions with your name on them, the associated stress, and the time away from home. Being looked after is just one small way of keeping you fresh and focused.

Speaking of home, you have to be thankful for your understanding spouse and forgiving kids. You know you don't see them enough, but the money compensates: they're well looked after. Nice home, the best schools, great holidays. And anyway, at this rate you'll be financially independent in just a few years and then you'll be able to spend much more time with them.

Your life is like riding a bike down a mountain road at top speed. You're pedalling as fast as you can, braking only enough before each corner to negotiate it safely. Then you pedal like mad again to rebuild your speed. To slow down too much would be a sign of weakness – it might allow someone else to catch up. To think about what you're doing, or why you're doing it, for more than the briefest moment would be to risk bringing your ride to a premature and probably messy end. You've worked hard and earned the right to be here. It wasn't dumb luck. And anyway, it is a lot of fun. Why would you want to stop?

In December 2001 this is the dream I was living, and had been living for a decade. I was enjoying the ride. A month later I was lying in a hospital bed, my head shaved and a surgeon's map drawn neatly onto my scalp with a permanent marker. Over the next twenty-four hours there was a chance I would lose my ability to speak, receive permanent damage to my brain, or even die. And if I was fortunate enough that none of those happened – that the brain tumour was successfully removed – I still faced the likely prospect of death within two or three years.

The trouble with travelling at high speed is that you can't do it if you think about it. Thinking causes hesitation, which causes uncertainty, and that's a recipe for failure. Back at my desk only five months after surgery, I found myself hesitating. It quickly became clear that I was not going to be able to get back on the bike. I had been changed by cancer.

I decided to take a year off at this point to work myself out, and came away with a completely different perspective on my work. In time, I would find myself grateful for this change in outlook (though not as grateful as one corporate friend might have been – he commented to me that I was 'lucky to have the opportunity to take time off to explore', seemingly forgetting the circumstances). Certainly my new level of consciousness – to use a term from the work I do now – has helped me build a more fulfilling life. Up to the point of my illness, I was ego centred – the world revolved around me – which at times led to arrogance and at other times to low self-confidence. Now, as will be explained fully, I am closer to what I call 'assertive humility'. That means having more care and compassion for both others and myself while my behaviour, decisions and expressed opinions are consistent with my values and beliefs. Assertive humility is an approach to life that is characterised by equanimity, not superiority or inferiority, and by presence with, not distance from, others. It comes with a sense of purpose and a sense of modesty. It is, simply, a more authentic way to be.

All of which conjures another interesting thought: What if I hadn't got sick? Would anything have changed or would I still be pedalling at the same crazy pace? Barring a life-threatening illness, what does it take to force a crazy-busy, work-absorbed person to question the wisdom of what they are doing?

These questions lie at the heart of this book. It is not a book that tries to make judgements about the high-end corporate lifestyle or anyone who is living it. As I've said, and will expand upon later, I've been there myself, enjoyed virtually every minute of it and completely understand its allure. Nor is this book a cancer survival story. I'll talk about my cancer and the fight against it, but largely in the context of what I learnt from the experience and the consciousness that was opened up as a result. For me, a very serious illness became a very serious wake-up call. My hope is that for you this book raises some of the same questions I faced – without the trauma.

There is one point I need to make before sharing my story. As we go, I'm also going to share, and explain, a model of consciousness that attempts to explain my shift from ego-centredness towards assertive humility. I believe this model has broad applicability and could also help you become a more conscious individual – someone who operates with less ego and more assertive humility. While it took a major disruption to my life for me to start to understand my consciousness, hopefully you will be able to do so without such a disruption.

When I started looking back over my life in preparation for this book, it seemed naturally to fall into a number of stages, defined roughly by four hats I wore along the way: from my Cub Scout hat to my Air Force officer hat to my corporate executive hat to my bandana. While these act to provide visual cues, it is not intended that the hats be seen as tying in with specific phases in the consciousness model I am presenting.

CHAPTER 1

Childhood:
the Cub Scout hat

'I could have put a spirit level on your bed when it was made; only later did I find out that you slithered in and out of it to keep it that way.' That's my mum talking, and her memory says a lot about the sort of child I was.

I was a straight kid. There's not really any other way of putting it. Obedient, eager to please, purposeful. When there were two chores shared between three of us – my older sister (Janine) and brother (Sean) and me – I was the one who worked out a third job so that we could have one each. I had the dubious habit of dobbing my brother or sister in to my parents rather than protecting them with a white lie. When something needed planning, I would make a list. I had lots and lots of lists. Put a goal in front of me and I would achieve it: I earned so many Cub Scout badges there was hardly any room on my uniform to add any more. A close family friend, who has known me all my life, summarises by describing my nature with a single word: 'discipline'.

In today's language I'd probably have been called a bit of a nerd too. My sister and brother remember me absorbing, in great detail, the rules of every game we ever owned and pulling out the more obscure ones at particularly annoying (for them) moments. At school I was far more thorough and studious than any other child.

There *was* plenty of fun and love in my life. Australian-born in the northern New South Wales town of Inverell in 1969, I grew up in the 'country', which meant a lot of time spent outdoors. Typical boy stuff like war games around my best mate's big backyard, playing golf, camping beside the dam and working as a ball boy for the Inverell Hawks rugby league team. I was fortunate to spend a lot of time with my dad, Geoff, golfing on weekends and with my grandfather on mum's side, George Brissett, helping out in his garage workshop and fixing 'stuff'. There were also plenty of family holidays, often to the coast to visit Dad's family.

What made me the earnest, rule-taking young person I became? Obviously my parents were a big influence, though they can't have been all of it as my brother and sister were both quite different to me (which I'll come back to shortly). Certainly there were many aspects of my early life that complemented and arguably bolstered the inherent aspects of my personality.

Both Mum and Dad balanced love and respect with strong discipline. Our home was run as a fairly tight regime underwritten by Catholic values. The wooden spoon (one was a souvenir from Sydney's Luna Park) was used to keep us in check if needed, not that I needed much of that. Mum stayed at home through most of my school years while Dad worked long hours running his butchery and smallgoods business. The strongest emotional connection was with Mum, and our relationship was pretty easy, due in no small part to my ready compliance. My relationship with Dad depended a lot on whether it was during the working week, when he was often stressed and sometimes angry, or on a weekend or holiday, when we would often do stuff together and he could be funny, generous and loving.

Pop Brissett was a big influence too, I think at least partly because he tended to treat me as an adult, or at least older than my years. That did lead to some dubious health and safety situations, including my hand being rammed by his boat against the dock while securing the line one time, and his dropping a spinning electric drill on my arm from a great height during a barbecue roof installation (I still have the scars to proudly show my kids). Another time – and this one was entirely my fault – I was working on a job with him and he realised he was missing a screwdriver. He asked me to ride my bike back to his house to get one. I sped away, eager to return in record time. By now my bike-riding skills had evolved to such a level of speed and intuition that I felt I only needed to listen at 'Give Way' signs rather than slow down and use my eyes as well. Riding back, screwdriver in hand and ears open, I sped through one of Inverell's busier intersections … and was hit by a car. I skimmed and skidded across the bitumen as if it were black ice and found myself lying on the ground in a world of blur and dull pain. I remember people scurrying all around, an ambulance, and the hospital. When my family arrived Janine took one look at me and fainted. The upshot was that poor old Pop felt terrible and my bike was a 'ride off'. I never did find out what happened to the screwdriver.

There were many other adults I looked up to, including the close family friend mentioned earlier and pretty much anyone else in a position of status: teachers, doctors, priests … you name it. Which probably explains my willingness to absorb the lessons of the Catholic church, both at school and at Mass. The church played nicely to my conformist, obedient value system. It must have been a positive experience or I'm not sure I would have been willing to take the frosty early morning rides to church with Sean to serve the six o'clock Mass as an altar boy.

Ego is a dirty word

Ego is something that each of us carries with us to some extent, though it can be particularly strong as a child. We can see ego as the protection, promotion and enhancement of artificial self-image. Recalling our own childhoods – and certainly my own – it's not hard to see the role that ego can play. Most teenagers – including those who pretend otherwise – are concerned about 'how I look' or 'what others will think', or about the embarrassment wrought by a parent doing or saying the wrong thing.

There is a multitude of perspectives on the term 'ego', how it is defined and how it is perceived in psychology and by the wider community.

Sigmund Freud coined the term 'ego' in the 1920s. He posited ego as one part of a psychic triad, alongside the 'id' and the 'superego', with ego pragmatically balancing tension between the external world, a desire for indulgence ('id') and an aspiration for morality ('superego').

Contemporary dictionary definitions define ego quite generally, around one's sense of self-esteem, though what we are discussing here (and throughout this book) is a more targeted notion of ego.

A more meaningful, if brutal, definition for our purposes might be that of the Buddhist teacher Sogyal Rinpoche in his 'must read' book, *The Tibetan Book of Living and Dying*. Sogyal defines ego as 'absence of true knowledge of who we really are, together with its result: a doomed clutching on, at all costs, to a cobbled-together and makeshift image of ourselves, an inevitable chameleon charlatan self that keeps changing, and has to, to keep alive the fiction of the existence'. In this sense ego is a much more primitive concept than the dictionary definitions allow, implying that ego represents something is 'missing' in one's self-development.

For the purposes of this book and for practicality of application, I have simplified Sogyal's definition. I define ego as *an over-inflated or under-inflated image of self, formed from self-judgement or perceived judgement of others, which masks our true essence.*

Clearly, ego can lead to a wide range of dysfunctional emotions and behaviours. We'll explore these in some detail later, but first let me demonstrate via three manifestations of my own ego in action in my early years.

Entitlement and judgement of others

Entitlement may not be something you would immediately associate with a middle-class family living in a country town, but entitlement is all relative. In fact there was quite a strong sense of entitlement running through our extended family. Pop Brissett was one of the first businessmen in Inverell; with his brother he started a bicycle shop then a car dealership – he brought the first motor cars to the town. Later he owned and ran a real estate agency. My dad ran his butcher shop for many years then later opened a retail furniture business that became the largest in the region. All in all, the Taylor and Brissett names were well known about town. I don't want to overplay this – we didn't see ourselves as royalty (except my grandmother, Nan Brissett, who did almost see herself as a local version of the Queen Mother) – but there's no doubt this sense of entitlement contributed to a feeling of having a worthy place in society.

It should be self-evident that entitlement can only exist in the presence of ego. It is fundamentally 'all about me in comparison to others'. Similarly, ego leads to judgement of others. The ego of my youth was clearly built on doing the right thing: my self-image depended on my ability to please, or at least to not displease. My brother and sister, particularly Janine, were quite different. It was with amazement, awe and tinges of contempt that I watched them continually pushing boundaries (as I saw them defined) with Mum and Dad. When Janine was about eighteen she started going out with a guy in his early twenties. Mum and Dad, particularly Dad, were not impressed. When it came to a head one night, with a huge shouting match, tears, yelling, rage – even the 'Get out and don't come back' line – the thirteen-year-old me sat in a corner with boggled eyes. I could not understand why Janine was willing to be so rebellious, and certainly looked on her in a dim light as a result. Needless to say, Janine and I did not get on well during this period.

In practice, entitlement and a tendency towards judgement were relatively mild aspects of my ego. Far more significant was perfectionism and, to a lesser extent, its sidekick: over-caring. These were prominent features of the youthful Stuart Taylor and would stay with me, in various guises, over quite a few years (and perhaps, to some extent, to this day).

Perfectionism

If the early signs of a strong perfectionist streak were there in the neatness of my bed, school was where I really gave it rein. I started school at the relatively young age of four and a half. By Grade Four I had become a highly dedicated student obsessed with success. My teacher in that year started giving out merit certificates for the best result in each subject and I set out to win as many as I could. I only remember missing out on two, and I did win the top-of-the-class award. I kept this up through the rest of primary school, eventually winning dux of pretty well every subject. To most of my peers I suspect I was seen as the smart, nerdy one.

In secondary school this just ramped up. I rushed home after my first day in Year Seven and dived straight into summarising the lessons of the day. In Year Ten, the final year at my Catholic school, I was both school captain and dux. Despite the disruption of having to move to the state high school to finish my schooling, I maintained the pressure on myself and topped years eleven and twelve there.

All of this dedication and commitment was entirely self-imposed and set against my own high standards. Where most mothers encourage their children towards their homework, my mum would encourage me away from mine, sending me outside to play. But my ego, manifesting in this perfectionism, was too strong to be held back.

Assertive Humility

There's nothing inherently wrong with seeking perfection. Aspiring for perfection is what drives outstanding performance, whether that be in sport, music or any other field of human endeavour. What's more, perfectionism doesn't impose pressure or expectations on others. It is characterised by pressure on yourself from within: the perfectionist tries to achieve 120 per cent because he or she wants to – not because someone else wants them to.

The personal downside of perfectionism comes from consistently applying *too much* pressure on yourself. Further, a strong attachment to this perfectionism can make it obsessive and unhealthy.

Engineers often use the 'pressure-performance curve' to describe structures and machines. The typical curve (Figure 1) shows performance rising with pressure (as, say, a car engine speeds up with increased input of fuel), up to a point. Beyond that point, however, performance drops away as the engine, in this example, begins to operate sub-optimally. If the pressure continues to be increased, the engine will eventually fail. (The engines of domestic vehicles rarely fail, as they operate well below their performance peak; race-car engines, which operate very close to that peak, often fail.)

A very similar model can be applied to human performance, both physical and mental. With zero pressure, there is little reason to achieve anything, so zero performance results. As pressure increases, so does performance. Most of us are familiar with the ability to stretch ourselves to unusual levels of focus and productivity as a deadline approaches: that's a sign that we're near the top of the pressure-performance curve.

Pressure performance stages

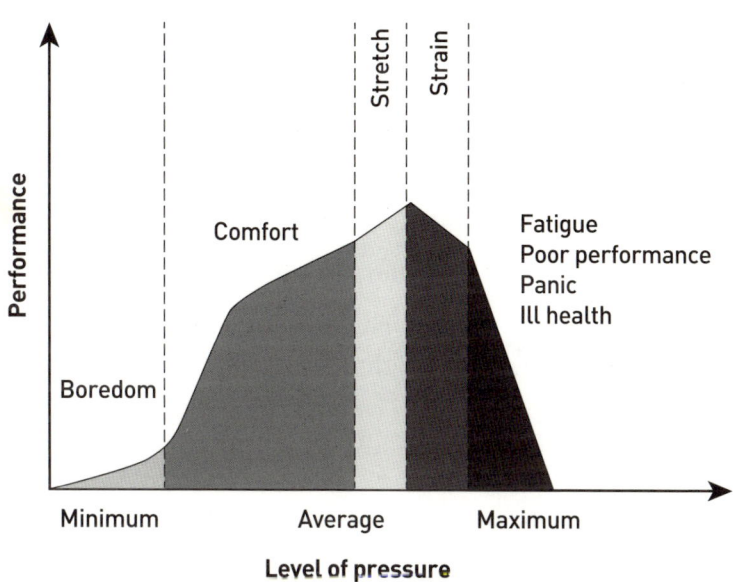

Figure 1: The Pressure – Performance Curve

Optimal performance occurs, naturally, right at the top of the curve. This is sometimes referred to as being 'in the zone', or being in a state of 'flow'. This is what athletes try to aim for in their most important events, such as an Olympic final. Their training regime aims to put the body, emotions and mind under just enough pressure that they are at peak fitness, positivity and focus just prior to their event. An athlete who is 'underdone' will fall short of their best due to insufficient pressure having been applied. By contrast, an athlete who has applied too much pressure – either physically through over-training or mentally through 'over-psyching' themselves – will also fall short of their best as they operate past the peak of the curve.

In terms of my school performance through most of my childhood, I think it's fair to say that I usually operated at close to peak performance from a cognitive perspective. I put myself under a lot of pressure, and saw any assignment or exam as my own personal Olympic final – and I achieved very good results. Along the way, however, there were signs that, with hindsight, could well have been the result of pushing myself too far. A bigger question mark was whether I had the emotional fitness to work with this pressure. For instance, I continued to wet the bed until I was eight years old, and I had a tendency to sleepwalk right into my teens. Later in my life, my propensity for perfectionism would cause me a great deal more stress.

Approval-seeking and judgement by others

As a boy I remember being highly attuned to the adults around me. As I said earlier, I was always eager to please and anxious not to displease. I found it hard to understand how my brother, Sean, seemed not to overly care about the views of others, especially those of Mum and Dad. In a way, I looked up to him for his self-guided approach.

Approval-seeking can be strongly related to perfectionism in that it results from a self-imposed, egocentric pressure to achieve. The difference is the source of pressure. Where perfectionism is associated with pressure from within – the need to score another personal best, irrespective of what others around you are doing – approval-seeking results from pressure sourced from the environment around you. When you combine the two, now you do have a cocktail for stress; a fear of failure. More than that, approval-seeking becomes an addiction, as it did for me. I loved getting the accolades, then I needed to get the accolades. I didn't get in trouble, then I didn't want to get in trouble.

Imagine a primary school teacher who hands you back a project and says, 'I loved the work you did on this – it was really great'. You're left feeling quite chuffed. The next day you submit another piece of work and wait in anticipation for the teacher to return it with similar enthusiasm. Only this time something changes: the teacher walks past you and picks out Sue, the little girl behind you, telling her that her project was the best in the classroom. Now your ego steps in and causes you to worry that the teacher didn't like your work this time, and maybe you're really not as good as you had thought. You must not let this happen next time!

Notice how in this case your feeling of self-worth is not determined by your own measure of your worth, but by the relative attention given to your work by your teacher. You are at the mercy of the environment – the teacher in this case, a boss in another, a parent in yet another – to provide you with positive reinforcement. Failure to get the sort of feedback you are looking for leads you to strive even harder in an attempt to get it next time. The pressure increases, which causes performance to also increase – in this sense caring about the views of others can obviously be a positive thing. But if the pressure goes too high, caring becomes approval-seeking … you know the rest.

To return to the earlier example of the athlete: approval-seeking can result from excessive media attention, or perhaps from an overwrought rivalry with another athlete. Both increase the pressure to perform, on top of any pressure applied by the athlete him or her self.

In my later teens, my tendency to over-care declined, though it never entirely left me and it would return with some fervour in the not-too-distant future.

Forms of ego

Entitlement and judgement, perfectionism and approval-seeking are all behaviours associated with different forms of ego. Each of them I can recognise in my past, particularly in my youth, though elements were carried on into adulthood as well, as we shall see.

Figure 2 outlines the full diversity of ego as I recognise it today. My reflections on my own experience, along with observations I have made and the understanding I have sought from experts over the last decade, have led me to construct this model. I divide it into two sections on one axis – over-care and under-care (or 'don't care') – and two sections on the other axis: 'about me' and 'about others'.

Consciousness and Personal Growth

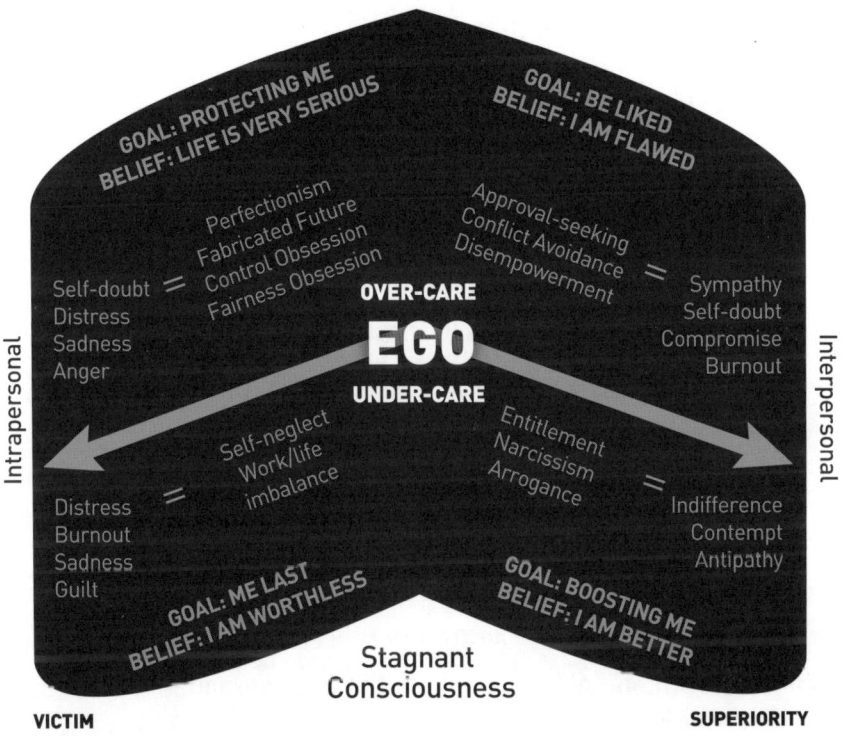

Figure 2: Forms of ego

Over-caring is exactly what I was demonstrating via the perfectionism and approval-seeking just discussed. In many ways these are the same thing, perfectionism being based on self-judgement and approval-seeking being based on the judgements of others.

When I over-care about self I can find myself operating with a range of *obsessions*, including (but not limited to) the following. At times I have demonstrated all of these:

- a need to be perfect and not fail, i.e. the perfectionism we have just explored

- the need to control my environment

- an inflexible view that my negativity about the future is accurate and any imagined threat must accordingly be treated as real

- a deep requirement that life must be fair.

Over time these obsessions feed on themselves, become reinforced and burn neural pathways into the brain. With them on board, the worldview becomes a very serious perspective that can lead to a lot of internal turmoil, including self-doubt, anxiety, sadness and anger.

The other side of over-caring is that focused on the judgements of others: *dependency*. My approval-seeking was a good example. Other aspects of dependency I have personally been less prone to, but have witnessed in others, are conflict avoidance and disempowerment. An unhealthy dependency forms in relationships when one over-cares about others and their opinions, values, possessions and performance. The measurement of self-worth is now relative and external rather than based on 'personal best' and values. A need for approval and constant affirmation from others drives a very cautious approach to social interactions. It stifles self-confidence, destroying creativity and ensuring withholding expression of original opinions. Associated with this can be avoidance of, or at least huge discomfort with, conflict – for fear it may 'rock the boat' or ruin existing (unhealthy) relationships. For emerging leaders this can be an impenetrable glass ceiling; for existing leaders it can render them ineffective. This also manifests as a driver for someone being sympathetic to another person. With sympathy, the superficial, observable motivation is a caring person. However, eventually the true colours of the interaction reveal disempowerment, compromise and conflict avoidance. The sympathetic person doesn't help the other person move forward. Rather, they potentially deepen their pain. Over time the over-caring person/leader can be seen as weak and part of the problem. The disempowering aspect of this interaction means that the over-carer is at risk of overload and burnout.

The 'flip side' of ego is under-caring. This can manifest as *detachment* on the 'about others' side of the scale, and *self-neglect* on the 'about me' side.

Superficially it can be hard to see how under-caring about self – self-neglect – can be egotistical. However, its underlying belief of 'I am worthless' is the martyr's view of the self. A person displaying this type of ego is unconsciously saying, 'I am so important that it is essential that I sacrifice myself; the way I emphasise that importance is to appear to not care about my own welfare'. Alternatively, under-caring about self can be a mirror image of over-caring about others. This is not an unusual situation for those in traditional carer roles, both professionally (e.g. nurses, HR professionals) or in relationships (e.g. mothers).

When we under-care about self, the toll increasingly shows. Lack of exercise, sub-optimal sleep and poor nutrition can become habitual and normal. This would become a common experience of mine later in my corporate career. The human body is amazing at operating under physical fatigue, duress and neglect – particularly in one's younger years. After a while, and certainly as one ages, this no longer holds true. However, this decline is irrelevant when external success and achievement are the top priorities and health and longevity are unimportant. 'I'll exercise tomorrow' or 'I haven't got time to exercise today' become the norm. The associated consequences are poor sleep, distress and sickness, as well as guilt and sadness.

The contrasting form of under-caring is detachment – a 'don't care about others' form of ego, where the goal is about boosting one's self-esteem at the expense of others. Detachment is associated with those behaviours perhaps most commonly associated with ego, such as arrogance, contempt and narcissism, as well as entitlement, as discussed.

When we under-care about others, we emotionally detach from the vast population of people, only maintaining relationships with those who are in our inner sanctum or who represent a means to achieving our goals. We start to regard others as 'it', 'its', 'they', 'those people'. We believe that we are entitled, a 'cut above the rest' and expect special treatment whenever we interact with the world. Other people are lesser in terms of opinion, values, performance, possessions and stature. In reality, we have an inflated self-opinion that feeds on itself. The resulting interaction is one of indifference, contempt or antipathy. In many cases the ego-centric element of under-caring about others is as much about protecting against an underlying frailty. In others words, the best defence is offence.

Assertive Humility

CHAPTER 2

ADFA and RAAF: the Air Force hat

Assertive Humility

In 1987 I left behind the Cub hat of my childhood and moved to Canberra to attend the Australian Defence Force Academy (ADFA). My new hat would be that of the Royal Australian Air Force (RAAF) officer. There are few more significant steps in a young person's life than leaving home. Moving a distance away, and into an environment like ADFA, forced on me a very rapid transition from boyhood to manhood. I don't think there was a significant shift in my consciousness level initially. In many ways the inherent discipline of the armed forces played directly to my rule-taker tendencies – though I have no doubt that ADFA represented a tipping point.

I had applied to ADFA not because I had watched too many war movies, nor even had dreams of seeing front-line action, but because I was sold by their heavy marketing at the time: glossy brochures and ads, the promise of 'a good start to your career', and the idea of being paid to study. Perhaps I should have watched more movies, particularly those portraying boot camps, because to a large extent I was caught by surprise by the intensity of the six weeks of training that preceded the first university semester. They were at once surreal and awful … and amazing.

It started from the moment we got off the bus.

The third-year cadets, having survived their first two years, were now in charge – and they were champing at the bit to get their own back. And they had seen the boot camp movies. So there was yelling and screaming. Do this! Do that! Wake-up calls at five in the morning. Scrubbing of toilets and bathrooms, cleaning the blocks.

Ironing of uniforms with enough starch to make them stand on their own with no 'railroad tracks' (double creases). Spit-polishing boots to a mirror finish, and then some more. The trick was to get your appearance to a standard high enough that you would not stand out on parade.

Of course there were plenty of rules for me to abide by, though there was a subtle difference from my past in that some of the rules were unwritten, and imposed by peers rather than superiors. So while Rules 1 and 2 of parade were 'Never turn up late' and 'Always be dressed to a perfect standard', Rule 3, which took absolute precedence, was 'Never turn up to parade without your mates'. While Rule 3 meant occasionally breaking Rule 1, the punishment was sweeter knowing you'd broken a rule by being a team player. The spectacle created by the third-year cadets if a first year turned up having broken Rule 3 was something to be avoided at all costs.

Despite the initial shock of that first six weeks, I survived and, for the most part, thrived through it. The pressure was something entirely different from what I had been placed under in the past. Looking back, both perfectionism and over-caring were encouraged: aside from the very high dress standards and an expectation that orders would be obeyed without question, our rooms needed to be kept to inspection standard (i.e. perfect), zero dust on all horizontal surfaces, hospital corners on beds made so tightly you could bounce a sock and hit the ceiling, waste-paper bins constantly empty, clothes baskets likewise, sock drawers with all socks lined up and smiling. The levels of tidiness must have been a shock to those of my mates more used to living in a typical teenager's bedroom. By contrast, my 'familiarity' with high standards probably helped me cope: it was a 'black and white' world and I'd spent my life being a 'black and white' person. Once the university year kicked off, the intensity of military life diminished a little. The academic pressure of an engineering degree picked up and filled the void, with 34 contact hours per week and high expectations on all of us to achieve good results. But this was right in my comfort zone. Though my wife now laughs at me whenever I say this, I remember looking forward to the exam timetables coming out and the chance to 'strut my stuff'.

The year-end at ADFA is marked by a graduation parade. It's a big deal, involving weeks of marching practice and preparation of uniforms to an even higher standard than usual. My parents attended, as did Nan and Pop Brissett. It was very special for Pop, as he had an Air Force background himself: he was a Leading Aircraftman during World War II, serving in New Guinea as an aircraft mechanic in 75 Squadron.

As a first-year cadet, one of the challenges of the parade is to 'present arms' to the graduating class (third years) as they 'slow-marched' around the enormous parade ground. This meant holding an L1A1 7.62mm Self-Loading Rifle (SLR), weighing a seemingly light four kilograms, vertically and at arm's length in front of your body, standing perfectly still, during the entire march. By the way, the rifle had bayonet engaged. The process took about fifteen minutes, but it felt like hours. As the minutes passed, it was easy for the mind to start playing tricks as the weight bore down. It was not unusual for a first-year cadet to faint during the presenting of arms, performing what is called the 'bacon dance' – more of a wobble – as they seek to maintain their position in a delirious state before falling to the ground. Fainting doesn't go down well – it is seen as a sign of disrespect for the graduating class and a sign of mental, emotional and physical weakness, not to mention the danger of a lethal weapon with an out-of-control bayonet on its end. There was no way I was going to embarrass myself in this way (a good example of over-caring), so with my usual dedication to preparation, I had well and truly mastered the art and endurance of presenting arms well before the day.

A highlight of my second year at ADFA came at the end of that year. We were sent into the bush on the 'Cryptic Challenge', an intense exercise designed to test our leadership and resilience. The exercise involved walking about 100 kilometres over four days carrying a full pack and webbing (extra equipment strapped around the body). At random times orders were delivered to us to complete some sort of urgent mission: rescuing a downed pilot, retrieving a trailer from a creek, finding our way to designated co-ordinates for a food drop. For each mission a different member of our group was assigned as leader – it was a real-time opportunity to explore the experience of leading others while under physical and psychological pressure. With little food and almost no sleep over the four days, the pressure really started to pile on by day three. A few in our group started to crumble at this point and we had to pull together to keep the group solid and spirits up. A strong team spirit, plenty of humour and positivity (to the tune of *Don't Worry, Be Happy*) kept us going. Walking out of the theatre of operations towards the finish line, side by side, was highly fulfilling. It was really only in that last kilometre or so that my body started to share its pain. It was a powerful exercise, with many lessons of leadership that continue to influence my thinking today.

At the beginning of third year, the aeronautical engineers were moved down to RAAF Point Cook in Victoria to attend Royal Melbourne Institute of Technology (RMIT) for our final two years of the degree. In spite of attempts by appointed RAAF Squadron Leaders to enforce a discipline, nothing could compare to our ADFA regime and so we settled into a relative 'Club Med' existence, attending RMIT with non-military people. Not to mention the Melbourne nightlife clearly towered over anything Canberra could hope to offer for extracurricular activity.

From this group of RAAF, Navy and Army guys came lifelong friends. Twenty-five years down the track, I am still in touch with many from this group. There is nothing liked shared challenges/ adversity and a 'common enemy' (read third-year cadets, drill sergeants, the institution) to forge deep, deep friendships.

Stress and the fabricated-future obsession

There can't be many environments more testing to the ego than defence force cadet training. While, as I've said, ego in the form of perfectionism and approval-seeking were effectively encouraged at ADFA, and self-confidence was seen as a positive thing, any hint of ego manifested as arrogance was quickly beaten out of you. On one occasion in first year I must have crossed this line. I don't remember the exact circumstances, but the result was that my room was 'bished' (rubbished) by a group of second years: everything in the room was upturned, to the extent that tidying up was at least a three-hour job. This sort of thing ensured that one didn't under-care about the hierarchy as you tried to carefully navigate your way without slipping into arrogance.

In this sense, the ADFA and RAAF environments were a study in stress.

We all suffer stress from time to time. Stress about school, stress about fitting in, stress about relationships, stress about workload, stress about being stuck in traffic or running late. The symptoms of stress are real and physical, and they can be serious. Some learn to live with it or manage it; others thrive on it; others suffer through its accumulation, sometimes to the point of becoming ill as a result.

Most of us go through life being aware of stress but having very little understanding of what drives it. Even if we do take the time to think about it (which admittedly I didn't do for many years, not having the time or the stress-free headspace), the triggers for stress seem so many and varied that pinning down a cause appears to be a fruitless task. That's because we see stress as being triggered by the environment in which it occurs: the office, the traffic, a relationship, and so on.

Coming back to Figure 1 on page 17, stress is fairly easy to understand if we look at it in the context of ego, or protection of self-image. Stress is closely aligned to a belief system that forecasts a future in which our self-image will somehow be damaged. I call this the 'fabricated future'.

My childhood was particularly prone to stress on this basis, as I've explained, given my propensity for perfectionism and over-caring. So I would get stressed by the thought of potentially missing out on a merit certificate. I would get stressed by the thought of disappointing my parents in some way. I would get stressed ahead of exams. All this stress caused me to pile the pressure on myself, making me work harder and harder and pushing me further and further up (and then over) the pressure-performance curve. What I now understand is that it wasn't the external pressure that was causing the stress – it was my fabricating of a future in which 'failure' would damage my self-image.

Exactly the same emotional situation plays out in our everyday lives. Recently I was scheduled to give a one-day workshop on resilience and high performance to a group of engineers from a division of a large CBD-based corporate client. I headed out to the suburban office of the division; it was not far from my home and I hadn't been there before, so I arrived a good thirty minutes before the scheduled start time of nine o'clock. As the start time approached I was concerned that no one seemed to be arriving. I called my contact's mobile and left a message; he called me back a few minutes later to say that they were all waiting for me … in the city office. So here I was, my audience of time-conscious engineers twiddling their thumbs a good half-hour away at best. It's a classic everyday stress scenario, the response to which could have been a hasty drive, every red light, a flustered arrival and a below-par workshop. Only this time I knew better. I recognised that the source of my stress in this situation was not the act of arriving late – it was the fear that I would look unprofessional and thereby damage my image. It was a fabricated future in which these engineers would think less of me because of the mix up. Turning the situation around in my mind, I was able to rationalise it as 'just one of those things'. The reality was that everyone in the room had been through a similar situation of their own at some stage, and they fully understood that these things happen. None of them was going to think less of me if I arrived late but ready to go, and then ran a good workshop. Chances were that if I just got on with the job, the late start would be a distant memory by morning tea. In short: that fabricated future was never going to happen, so therefore I didn't need to distress myself. I drove calmly to the correct venue, engaging positive emotions while I did so, and ran a successful workshop.

And this is an important point: the thing about forecasts – 'fabricated futures' – is that in the vast majority of cases they never happen or they are wrong. We feel stress in traffic because we think we'll look silly being late, yet five minutes after we arrive no one gives our lateness another thought. We feel stress about 'having a lot on', when in reality the source of that stress is concern that people will think less of us if we don't deliver – and of course in 90 per cent of cases we do deliver (and even if we don't there are pressure releases available, such as the renegotiation of deadlines ahead of time). Most people have had the experience of lying awake at three or four o'clock in the morning worrying about some situation that faces them the next day and (usually unconsciously) how their reputation might be tarnished as a result. In the cold, hard light of day those early-hour imaginings never come to fruition, the reality of the situation proving far more innocuous, with reputations – and egos – remaining intact.

With hindsight I can now see that the ADFA environment was manipulating pressure levels in order that we would learn about living with that pressure, build our confidence and equanimity while having any sharp edges knocked off our egos, and experience the need to balance ego and humility. It was largely fear of repercussions that drove our striving for perfection in those first few weeks and onward. While those repercussions were relatively trivial (such as the 'bishing' of a room, or marching up and down the square), they were aimed squarely at our egos. The fear of looking like a fool, of being brought down a couple of pegs in front of our peers, was a far more meaningful threat than any physical consequences.

This is balanced by a level of forced humility, whereby things like 'Rule 3' ensure that while keeping your focus on yourself is important, you always have one eye on your mates and how they are going as well. I'm sure that by the time we graduated from ADFA after three years, the defence force would have liked that humility to take centre stage – for us to have become humble young officers ready to lead with respect and learn from the rank and file. It didn't necessarily turn out that way for all.

Assertive Humility

Having completed officer training and a university degree in aeronautical engineering, I moved into the Air Force proper at the RAAF base at Amberley, outside Brisbane in Queensland. My role was as a junior officer, which meant that after an initial period of mentoring by another (second-year) officer, I would take responsibility for a unit of my own. I had plenty of confidence – ADFA had ensured we all had that – though I also harboured a number of doubts. The challenge would be whether I could temper that confidence and use it productively.

It might be useful at this point to briefly explain the culture and hierarchy of the Australian Defence Force. People enter the force – in my case the RAAF branch of it – either directly through the defence force recruitment process as an airman, or through officer training via ADFA. ADFA graduates enter their chosen branch at the level of junior officer. At their first posting they are eventually put in charge of a 'flight' of airmen, ranging from the rank of 'Aircraftsmen' (aged eighteen to twenty-five) to 'Warrant Officer' (aged forty to sixty). Being a junior officer is the armed forces equivalent of a university graduate going straight into a junior management role, managing others who may already have been in the business for some years – in the military case, people double and triple your age. As you can imagine, this creates some tension: ADFA graduates often ooze confidence, sometimes cockiness, while their subordinates, who are often quite a lot older and certainly more experienced, greet new officers with wariness. It's fair to say some ADFA graduates figured that having survived the training, they were now ready to run the place. We had some disdain for those above us in the senior officer ranks, who we often saw as incompetent. It's fair to say, too, with the benefit of hindsight, that we were very green.

So in a fairly short time I was standing up in front of my own unit with, to be quite frank, no idea what I was doing. All the leadership training in the world prepares you very little for the realities of actually taking charge of people who have, in some cases, over thirty years experience in their roles, not to mention vastly more life experience. My warrant officer – my direct report and traditionally an 'old hand' who can provide quiet guidance on the side – happened to be also new and relatively inexperienced. He'd come from an office environment and this was his first operational role, and while he was very enthusiastic and supportive, he just didn't have the established power base of some of his older equivalents. So all in all there was very little respect for either of us coming from the rest of the unit. There is sometimes an assumption in the wider community that the discipline and hierarchy of the defence forces create automatic respect for rank. That is not the case. Respect has to be earned, as it does in any other area of life – and I had a lot of earning to do.

For me, this was a situation primed for stress as a result of over-caring. While I maintained my outward confidence, perhaps with a tinge of arrogance from time to time, I had plenty of internal anxiety about whether I was up to the job (and fabrication of a future in which I wasn't, and failed in some way). While I saw some of my fellow ADFA graduates mastering their new leadership role, it was clear that ADFA confidence alone wasn't going to cut it. Other graduates really struggled to achieve anything because they failed

to gain the respect of their troops. I couldn't wait for life experience
to catch up either: I remember having a conversation with one
of the senior troops in my unit about some marital issues he was
facing, and here was I in my early twenties having had a handful
of girlfriends. The only real antidote to the stress was going to be a
curbing of my ego, allowing me room for less over-caring and the
corresponding development of a bit of humility. Thankfully for me
the early mentoring of the second-year officer was instrumental
in helping me to slowly build respect within my unit. He was an
outstanding leader, someone who exemplified a good balance of
self-assurance and humility – someone who did not over-care what
others thought about him but would also support his own troops
to the hilt. Today I would call his style compassionate leadership,
though at the time I understood it only as something to aspire to. In
the end I think I earned a degree of respect from my unit, though
I was a way off having the sort of relationship with them that
someone like that officer had with his. I was able to build a much
greater level of respect and confidence from my next opportunity –
one that would be pivotal to the next few years of my career.

In 1991 the Australian government launched the Commercial
Support Program (CSP), an initiative aimed at ensuring that 'non-
core' support services within the defence force were sourced in
the most cost-effective way. This opened the door for commercial
contractors to provide these services but, as part of the program,
units currently providing the services were permitted to submit
a competitive 'in-house' bid. I was given the role of leading the
submission for my unit, and with a contingent of my troops
seconded to the project, we set about planning a redesign of the

unit's work (which related to overhaul of F111 jet engines) in order to make it commercially viable. The project would introduce me to a different, much more positive, form of stress.

There were two significant aspects to this task from my point of view.

First, I finally found myself on a level with the troops working for me. While some of them were highly experienced in their day-to-day roles, as we embarked on this very large project none of us had any significant experience in either process re-engineering or commercial tendering – we were all at the same starting point and I no longer needed to over-care. I remember one Flight Sergeant with years of experience but who could hardly write and was very challenged by the redesign task; I was able to work with him, tapping into his knowledge and coaching him as he wrote up his part of the bid. Far from over-caring, I was now able to work with a degree of compassion that had been foreign to me.

Second, we were provided with the assistance of some external consultants. Having had no corporate exposure whatsoever by this point in my life I had no concept of management consulting. Working with these people as they challenged our blinkered 'military' perspective and opened our thinking to new, possible ways of working was a revelation to me. It was like doing a compressed MBA. In a way they introduced me to a new kind of 'perfect': the idea of the perfect way of working.

As the submission date for bids got closer, the workload on our project ramped up and the pressure, and stress, piled on. It wasn't about winning at this stage – it was simply about getting our bid across the line. We worked increasingly long hours, including at least one 'all nighter' driven, in the language I've been using, by a shared fabricated future in which we failed to finish on time. But this was positive stress. While we pushed our performance right up to the maximum, I don't think we ever let the pressure push us over the hump and into failure territory. Further – and this is an important point – our stress was kept positive by our measuring of ourselves only against ourselves: we weren't competing with the other bids; we were just getting the best bid in that we possibly could. It was the equivalent of an athlete who only ever measures his or her performance against a personal best, as opposed to a win-loss ratio.

Our submission was followed by physical and emotional exhaustion, but also a feeling of euphoria at what we had managed to achieve. It was something so far away from what any of us would initially have imagined possible. When we eventually learnt that our bid had actually won, beating the commercial tenderers, there was even more satisfaction, though I don't think as much as we got from completing the bid in the first place. As a post script to this story, twelve months after this process the government of the day decided they didn't want to keep this service in-house after all and it was outsourced.

Leading this process gave me a substantial confidence boost, as did the chance to work with some really proficient external consultants.

The experience would soon become a catalyst for my move to civilian life, a corporate career … and a lot more stress.

Fairness obsession

If the move away from home to ADFA signalled a shift in consciousness (albeit one of which I was unaware at the time), an event in early 1991 would really give that shift some impetus.

Just after Christmas in 1990, while I was home in Inverell on leave, my father had a heart attack. Dad had always worked very hard and operated under high levels of pressure running his small businesses. He had been a heavy smoker and was overweight and unfit. Nevertheless, he was only forty-nine years old. He was admitted to the hospital in Inverell then airlifted to the regional hospital in Armidale, 120 kilometres to the south.

All of us travelled down the highway to be with him. Dad was asleep when we arrived at the hospital, so we were asked to stay in a waiting room down the corridor. After a time Sean and I decided to go and see if he had woken up yet, leaving Mum behind. As we walked towards his ward, there was a commotion in front of us. A group of staff were on the floor working on a patient with CPR and a defibrillator. Within seconds we realised that the patient was our father. Apparently he had been walking down to see us and suffered another large cardiac arrest.

Before my eyes, I saw my father die.

As this was happening, the lift door opened nearby and my sister, Janine, eight months pregnant, stepped out onto the floor. Three of us were left standing there in shock. Then we had to return and break the news to Mum.

I was twenty-one years old when Dad died. To that point in my life nothing really sad, dramatic, shocking or traumatic had ever happened to me. I vaguely remember driving back to Inverell – we had a few cars in Armidale, so I had to drive on my own, in convoy with the family. Mainly it was just a blur, and a feeling of numbness. The deep sadness and anguish that followed Dad's sudden and premature death would stay with me for the next two years and beyond; the feelings return even as I write and re-read these paragraphs.

The pursuit and defence of the notion that 'life should be fair' is one of the most destructive practices a person can have. It causes an enormous amount of anger – dysfunctional, non-productive anger – in many people's lives. Unfortunately, the more we pursue the idea, the more angry, sad and disappointed we become.

We can expect fairness in a whole range of different situations. Expecting umpires to get it right every time in a sporting contest. Expecting the traffic to clear when we are in a hurry to get home. Expecting promotions always to be handed out on merit alone. Expecting those around us to live full lives to a ripe old age.

The early death of my father was a brutal wake-up call. I could reasonably say that up to that point life for me had been fair: a loving family, a good education, good health and plenty of opportunity. Perhaps because of this I hadn't given the concept of fairness a lot of thought. What Dad's passing did was give me a new reference point: from then on, whenever I have found myself in a situation thinking that 'life should be fair' – and there have been a number – I have been able to remind myself that it isn't. Similarly, I became more aware of the prevalence of this type of thinking in the wider population, and the unnecessary anger and sadness that results. There is simply no logic that can support such a belief.

This is not to discount the grief associated with the loss of someone close to you, or the disappointment and frustration that we all experience at times when things don't go our way. However, acknowledging that life isn't fundamentally fair means we can approach these situations in a more positive way. Instead of focusing our energy on a perceived inequity, we can focus on looking ahead, on making peace and taking action, on asking ourselves, 'How am I going to let this affect me?' We can focus on making choices.

Stagnant consciousness

During my years studying aeronautical engineering at ADFA, I started seriously questioning, and ultimately rejecting, my Catholic beliefs. I had been a very good Catholic as a youngster – recall those early-morning bicycle rides to act as an altar boy. But immersed in a highly rational, evidence-based discipline like engineering – which played directly to my 'black and white' nature – I found myself no longer able to accept what I saw as the almost fairytale nature of religious teachings in general and Catholic teachings specifically. Ultimately the combination of studying engineering, living and studying in the defence force, and then the death of my father, suppressed any semblance of spirituality as part of my character. It wasn't the values of Christianity that I was shrugging off, but rather I was becoming increasingly achievement focused, which left little room for the 'soft' stuff. Along with the mothballing of my spiritual radar, my consciousness was stagnating.

There are numerous models for articulating world views, human consciousness and human growth. One such model, developed by Clare Graves and published by Don Beck and Chris Cowan, is called Spiral Dynamics. Spiral Dynamics is a theory of human development that posits that human nature is not fixed but rather develops in line with circumstances. I don't intend going into a long-winded explanation of the theory here; suffice to say that it matches levels of consciousness with different life stages, maturity stages or perspective stages. It articulates how different people, ages and cultures have different and evolving conceptual models of reality.

Consciousness is (according to American author Ken Wilbur) 'an awareness of one's inner and outer world; mentally perceptive, awake, mindful'. We might say that one's level of awareness, in this sense, aligns with one's level of consciousness.

Typically a person's level of consciousness begins at the ego level (see Figure 3), in one or more of the various forms I have discussed. (A baby, to take an extreme example, has a fully self-centred view of the world, which is essentially based on the same survival instinct as any other animal's.) From here, consciousness will either stagnate or it will emerge/evolve as we age, as our circumstances change and as we become more self-aware.

Consciousness and Personal Growth

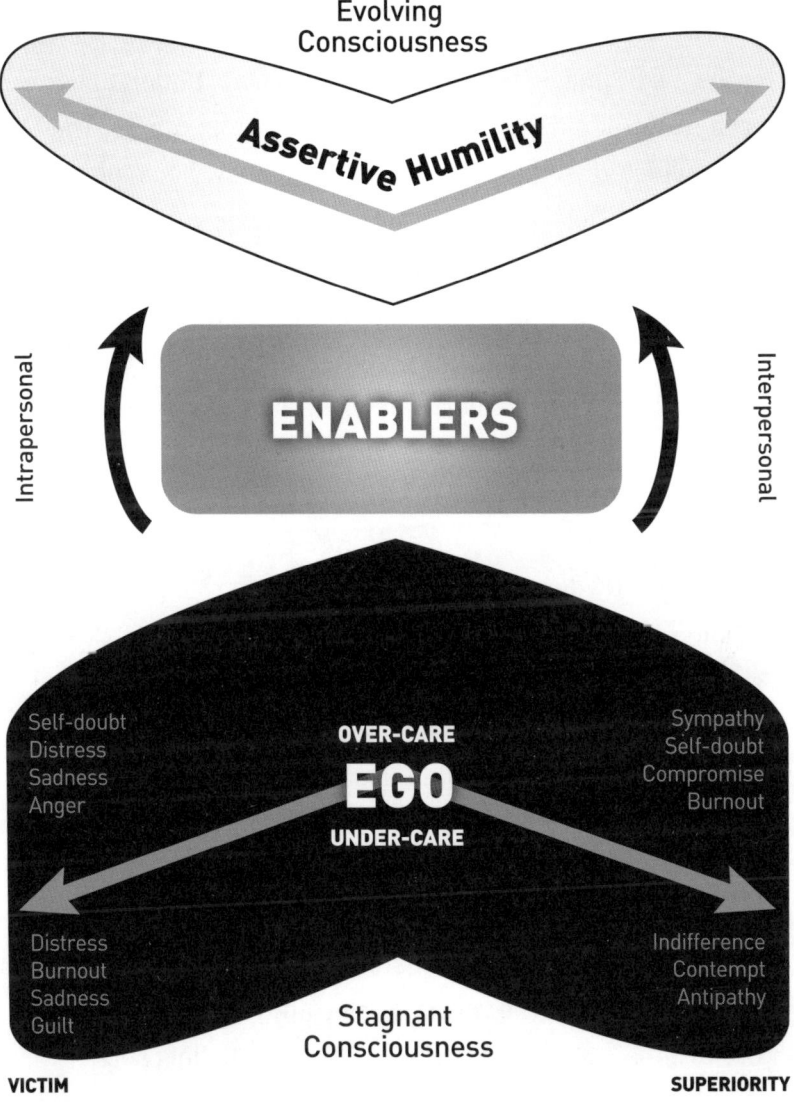

Figure 3: From stagnant consciousness towards evolving consciousness

Where consciousness evolves, ego tends to soften – a person can become humbler and live truer to their authentic self. We become more aware of the contribution we can make to the welfare of others, to the 'greater good' or the 'greater we', and less preoccupied with our own self-image, the need to make a contribution to the 'greater me' and/or a dependence on approval from others. The speed with which this happens varies enormously. Some people reach quite high levels of humility at a young age; some people never get much beyond the ego of their childhood, or even go backwards. Along the way there are a number of factors that can contribute to – enable – this shift or, under different circumstances, block progress. Perhaps the best way to explain this is to draw, again, on my own experiences.

Beliefs and choices

Not far from my home is a notorious intersection between two busy roads and a major suburban railway line. The volume of road and rail traffic through this area can lead to long delays – waits of as much as twenty minutes are not unusual at peak hour. Needless to say, a typical trip through this intersection can leave a driver with a high level of frustration and anger. I will admit that more than once I have arrived home in a foul mood caused entirely by the logjam. Or so I said to anyone who would listen. The reality is that my mood in this instance was not the result of the traffic at all. It was the result of my beliefs about the traffic at the time. Beliefs such as 'I've paid my registration so they should have done something about this mess' or 'I have a right to get home on time' or, ultimately, 'Life should be fair'.

An alternative response – one that I succeed in mustering more often today – is to accept the traffic for what it is and to go with the flow. My belief in this instance is that the traffic will be what it will be, and there's little I can do to fix it. So I turn up the radio, or put on some nice music, and block out the outside world. In this instance, rather than allowing the environment to govern my mood, I take control of my response myself. I arrive home buoyed by something I've been listening to and in a very positive mood. The interesting thing here is that the situation outside the car is essentially the same in both cases: slow-moving traffic and a delayed trip home. All that has changed is my beliefs and the choices (in terms of my reaction) I made as a result of them.

In these two illustrations we see the way that beliefs can either block (in the first instance) or enable (in the second) our consciousness's ability to move past ego and towards humility.

The psychology behind this was understood in ancient times. In a modern context, Albert Ellis, the founder of cognitive behavioural therapies, developed the ABC model in the 1950s:

*Activating events + **B**eliefs = **C**onsequence (in the form of emotions and behaviours)*

So 'traffic plus "*they should fix this*" equals *anger*', whereas '*traffic* plus "*these things happen*" equals *calm*'. Same event, different outcome due to different beliefs.

That means that to change any dysfunctional emotions we may feel
– anger in traffic, frustration at work, envy, sadness, fear, and so on
– all we need to do is change our beliefs. Easy? Not necessarily. The
problem is that often our responses to common situations become
entrenched – our beliefs represent a collection of well-trodden
neural pathways in our brains (I mentioned this in Chapter 1) and
these pathways are followed virtually automatically. One of these
situations occurs (traffic) and 'click', we react without any conscious
thought (anger). When this happens we have effectively outsourced
our emotions to the environment and so have become victims of that
environment, our mood changing in response to changes around us
rather than our own conscious decisions.

Closely aligned with beliefs are the choices we make as a result of
them.

My mother-in-law, who we'll meet shortly, is fond of saying, 'It's
not what happens to you in life, it's how you choose to respond to
it'. The thing is that our belief systems, while well trodden, are not
permanent: they can be rewired. The key is to train ourselves to
choose our response, rather than allow it to happen automatically.
In practice that means, first, noticing a dysfunctional reaction to
a situation – a reaction that isn't in line with who we are or who
we want to be. Initially you will do this in retrospect; with practice
you'll be able to do it at the time. With awareness of this belief-
centred concept and the ABC model, you should be able to recognise
and question any beliefs ('Life should be fair') that are supporting
your automatic response. Then you can condition yourself to try and
apply a different belief ('Life isn't fair') next time a similar situation

arises. Eventually you will find yourself able to *choose* to feel or behave in a way that is consistent with the person you want to be.

The notion of choosing your response is central to the message of this book. While it is not something I was capable of doing, for the most part, to this point in my life, I have raised it here as it forms a critical boundary between the egocentric behaviours and beliefs we have discussed so far – perfectionism, over-caring, stress as a result of a fabricated future, 'Life isn't fair' – and the more productive, self-aware beliefs and behaviours we will discuss in coming chapters. Over the years when I was moving into corporate life, I stayed firmly on the egocentric side of this boundary.

There was one very positive choice I made around this time – one that would prove to be perhaps the best I would ever make.

In November of 1991 (the end of my first year in the RAAF) a 'Dining In Night' – a type of Air Force ball – was held at the Amberley base. Seated next to me was an attractive young woman called Peta, who was attending with friends. We fell into easy conversation. As it turned out, we had both grown up in the same region of New South Wales and her family had also lived in Inverell for a period. We worked out that our fathers had been in the same Apex club and had probably played basketball against each other at some stage. Peta's father had also died, though much earlier than mine. Her mother, Carol, had four children under six when she lost her husband. We found we had a lot to talk about – not just these family coincidences but all sorts of issues.

I may have been lacking in spirituality at this time, but did find it in myself to turn on a bit of romance. As a first date I took her to a John Williamson concert (basically Australian country music) – perhaps not the most romantic choice, but we enjoyed it. When Peta's birthday fell soon after the ball I sent her an enormous box of flowers, alerting Carol and Peta's younger sister, Kim, that something was up. After that Peta and I got together most weekends, she travelling up to Brisbane from her home on the Gold Coast. We were engaged within six months.

Two days before our wedding in September 1993, I managed to put my back out while carrying a clothes dryer up the stairs to our new apartment. I ended up completely laid up and missed my own buck's night – my brother and mates all told me they had a great time. On the wedding day my back really wasn't any better. Without the assistance of painkillers and a chiropractor who was one of our guests, the ceremony would probably have been postponed. It did go ahead, complete with military guard. Later at the reception our much-practised bridal waltz turned into more of a shuffle, with Peta doing a little jump where I should have been performing a spectacular lift.

In the first year of our marriage we lived in Brisbane. In 1994 Peta successfully applied for a job with Qantas, but the role was based in Sydney. With over a year left on my commission I did not have the option of discharge from the Air Force at this stage, but I did manage to gain a transfer to RAAF Richmond, on the outskirts of Sydney. There I was able to be involved with more re-engineering initiatives alongside people from the accounting and consulting firm, KPMG.

My introduction to consulting through the work at Amberley and with KPMG at Richmond – particularly the excitement and energy I got out of leading the CSP project – convinced me that this was what I should do after finishing with the Air Force. I started applying to major consulting firms with a view to landing a position to step into in early 1996, when my commission with the Air Force would be complete.

True to my perfectionist nature I left nothing to chance in this process. I targeted each of the top firms, including Anderson Consulting (now Accenture), Deloitte, A.T. Kearney, PricewaterhouseCoopers and, of course, KPMG. I researched each organisation as fully as I could, identified key people to approach and ended up doing countless interviews. I approached all this with a high level of confidence, bordering on arrogance, built up through both my ADFA training and RAAF experiences. My approach to interviews was as much about my interviewing them as it was them interviewing me.

Whatever I did worked, as I received three great offers. There followed painstaking consideration: one of the KPMG people I had been working with recalls a long, intense telephone conversation as I grilled him over the pros and cons of his organisation. In the end I did choose KPMG on the basis of a good offer and the fact that I knew several key people already. The only downside: they were based in Melbourne. That meant Peta and I would have to uproot ourselves again, and this time it was Peta looking for a transfer. She got one, to Qantas's Melbourne office. Our lives were about to fly off in a whole new direction.

CHAPTER 3

KPMG and Heinz: the corporate hat

Assertive Humility

I will never forget walking down the 'Paris end' of Collins Street in Melbourne towards the KPMG headquarters. I was wearing a fresh new suit and ready to take on the world. My Air Force hat had been left well behind – emotionally I had taken it off almost a year before, when I decided to leave. In its place was a corporate hat and a focus on 'high flying' success. This would be a period I would come to regard as my 'dash for cash'. My consciousness level, from a spiral dynamics perspective, was pure 'achievist', driven only by a desire to win – with winning defined by earnings and power. My confidence level, boosted further by having received multiple job offers, was in overdrive. I was determined to succeed and more than willing to put in the time and effort required. Which was a good thing, for I was about to be simultaneously thrown in the deep end and put on the fast track. It would be a hell of a ride.

At the time I joined KPMG they still had a substantial amount of work with the Australian Defence Force. They had also recruited a number of other ex-military staff, so the typical scenario was for defence people to work on defence jobs. I sensed that this was not where the better opportunities would be and asked to be allocated to corporate projects. And there was plenty of those too: this was the period leading up to 'Y2K' and when re-engineering was becoming popular. It was a consultant's buffet.

One of my first jobs was to travel to Sydney and review the processes of a transport company ahead of a merger. I was to meet with a senior manager and long-time employee of the company so that I could understand the issues and recommend a framework for the future. From a distance, and certainly from the perspective of this client, the situation was ludicrous. Here was I, whose trucking knowledge would fit on the back of an envelope, presenting as some sort of 'expert' to a veteran of the industry.

My first contact with the client was to call him and arrange a meeting. 'I start at five in the morning,' he said, 'and I have a slot at that time for us to meet. Will that work for you?' I suppressed a gulp and without hesitation replied that it was no problem – I would see him in his office at that time. Clearly a power play from him, but in hindsight understandable, given the circumstances.

Here was a situation ripe to test me. My perfectionist streak meant I had to prove myself to myself. My over-caring streak meant I had to prove myself to this highly contemptuous client. My fear of failure meant I was able to fabricate all sorts of worst-case futures, sending my stress levels to the stratosphere. And my ego told me that failure was not an option. So I prepared. I spent hours and hours preparing for this meeting, even though there was very little to prepare for – it was an exploratory meeting after all. My engineering sensibilities pushed me towards scratching out some sort of framework for discussion, and that's what I did. That rough framework saved the meeting: it became the main discussion point, moving the focus away from personalities and the client's contempt for my naivety. What could have been an extremely ugly meeting ended up being something of a success.

Soon after this episode the stakes got higher. KPMG won the job to expand the work that I and others had been doing in various isolated sections of this transport client. We would now take a look

at the organisation as a whole, with a view to structuring a 'reset' – a complete re-engineering of the company. The partner for whom I was working, and the leader of this project, decided that having survived that first dunk into the deep end, I could probably cope with more. She asked me if I would take on the leadership of the project – it would be the overall 'glue' role that brought together all the disciplines, including IT, finance, processes, strategy, marketing, and so on. I would have a team of about ten consultants working for me; my role would be to liaise with the senior management of the client.

Now let's get one thing straight here. There is no way I should have been in a position to take on this role. It was about as high stakes as it could get, involving a very large corporation and a million-dollar fee. My experience to this point was minimal to say the least. My exposure to corporate life was even less. But the circumstances were such that KPMG had so much work on at the time that they simply didn't have the luxury of making this appointment based on experience. The partner liked what I'd done in that first job, and liked what she'd seen much earlier on the RAAF Commercial Support Program project. (She told me once that she had been impressed right from the start when, as a member of the selection committee for the CSP project, I had apparently given her and her colleagues quite a grilling at interview.) She liked my positive attitude and confidence and decided to take a punt on me. So she asked me if I was up for it and, with another of those silent gulps, I said that I was willing to give it a crack, though I'd probably need some support.

'Right', she said immediately. 'You need to get down to the client right now. They've got a whole-of-executive meeting happening and I want you to sit in on it and get a feel for where things are going and what they want to achieve.'

So this really was going to be the deep end. Here I was heading for a meeting with a bunch of senior managers I had never met, on a mission that at least some of them were going to be opposed to, and this time without any preparation time at all. Perfectionism, over-caring, stress and ego were all about to be stretched to the limit.

Positivity

What trumped all of those essentially dysfunctional traits in this instance was the quality of positivity. I walked into the executive meeting of our logistics client carrying with me a briefcase full of self-assurance. I found it within myself to jump right in and lead a conversation about what the current situation was, and what it could look like in the future. My approach worked and we came away from that meeting on a positive note and ready to start the project in earnest.

A lot of research has been done into the power of positivity. A well-known academic in this area is American professor of psychology Barbara Fredrickson. Her work has shown that happy, high-performance people tend to have a ratio of positive to negative emotions of at least 2.9:1, that is, they are positive about three times as much as they are negative. Positivity and negativity in this sense can be both emotional and cognitive, cognitive positivity being what

is generally called optimism. Importantly, Fredrickson does see a place for negative emotions and thoughts: she does not suggest that a ratio of 2.9:0 (always positive – otherwise known as 'not human') is desirable, and nor is a ratio of, say, 30:1.

The positivity we are talking about here can be incredibly powerful. Looking back over the major phases of my life that we have discussed so far, I could identify a number of times where my perfectionism and over-caring might have tipped me over the edge of that pressure-performance curve and into the territory of declining performance, fatigue or ill health. I could have cracked under the (self-imposed) pressure at school, given up and coasted through. I could have done the same at ADFA on numerous occasions, either as a result of the pressure of occasional bullying or the high standards I again set myself in my studies. I could have collapsed emotionally from the stress imposed by being dropped into leadership of a unit at Amberley while still extremely green – quite a few did. But in each of these cases a fundamentally positive, confident outlook, perhaps sitting somewhere close to that Fredrickson ratio, was enough to keep me sitting towards the top of the pressure-performance curve.

This reveals a couple of interesting aspects of positivity.

The first is that positivity can be driven by ego (thus forming the other side of ego as a two-edged sword). Outward confidence in oneself, to the point of arrogance, sits neatly on the ego continuum I introduced earlier. It's fair to say that the fact that I ultimately came through each of the tests that was thrown at me, from school to

ADFA to RAAF, served to continuously build that confidence on my part. It gave me, in turn, the positivity to come through that early-morning meeting in my initial KPMG days. My own confidence helped me win the confidence of people like my KPMG partner, leading to the bigger consulting role where, once again, positivity pulled me through.

The second is that there is more to the positivity-negativity ratio than is apparent at first. My current work on resilience has helped me to identify that both positivity and negativity can be further categorised into 'functional' and 'dysfunctional' forms. Perhaps the best way to explain this is via an example, and a very good example would present itself some time after we started the major KPMG project.

As the transport project gathered pace I found myself in my element. The pressure was intense, as was the workload and the intellectual challenge. If I wasn't in a meeting or facilitating a workshop, I was on the phone. Constantly. There was a lot of travel, but it was always under good conditions, with top hotels and restaurants. There was a strong sense of being part of something big which, compared to the relative insularity of the Air Force, gave me the impression of a much broader field on which to play. I revelled in it. My positivity grew and grew. And then it was hit for six.

One day we sat down for a meeting with the client sponsor – the client executive whose role was to oversee our project from their point of view. He started the meeting by saying, 'We are a long way behind in this project. The IT proposal that was recently presented is not grounded in reality and I'm beginning to wonder if you guys have any clue what you're talking about. We're paying you hundreds of thousands of dollars and I don't think you know where things are up to and where they are going'. He continued in this vein for some time. He expressed severe doubts about whether the project could be completed satisfactorily, and said that he was on the verge of putting the whole project on hold unless it was quickly reset.

I held my own in the meeting but when we left I was shattered. Completely out of the blue, our million-dollar project was on the verge of being cancelled. My initial response was to beat myself up. My perfectionism was being severely challenged and, as had rarely happened to me ever before, I couldn't see a way out. For someone with a very strong sense of 'Failure is not an option', this was a crossroad. I felt more vulnerable than I had for a long time. I started fabricating a worst-case future and my stress peaked accordingly. My over-caring switched into hyperdrive as I imagined the humiliation of failure in front of my KPMG colleagues.

I sat down with a KPMG mentor, who had been providing me with support on this project. His experience immediately came to the fore. He encouraged me to look at the bigger picture, to understand that client disenchantment is not uncommon and, perhaps more importantly, is very rarely personal. 'He doesn't think you have a plan', he said. 'All you need to do is demonstrate that you have a plan and in a week or so it will all be back on track.'

This advice, not to mention the calm demeanour of my mentor, was a godsend. He shifted my perspective from imminent failure to potential recovery. Quite quickly I moved back into my comfort zone, which of course meant pedalling even harder in order to build a plan and solve this problem. Before long, just as my mentor had predicted, we were back on track. We implemented a stronger project management framework, a better system of communication and routine meetings. I was not going to allow myself or my project to lapse into complacency again.

What I understand today is that from a positivity/negativity standpoint, this experience took me through all four phases illustrated in Figure 4.

I started the transport project with enormous excitement, having been given the fantastic opportunity to lead the exercise. My positivity was tempered and contained by my lack of experience: there was a healthy dose of trepidation balancing out that excitement. At this point my positive to negative ratio was probably somewhere around Fredrickson's 2.9:1 level, and it was entirely on the functional side of this diagram.

Emotion	Functional (+ve impact on others, reach full potential, bounce back)	Dysfunctional (destructive, indulgent)
Positive	Joy Excitement Calm	Delusional joy Pride
Negative	Flatness; sadness Anger Trepidation	Pity party Depression Rage Phobias, panic, dread

Figure 4: Emotional Positivity and Functionality

Time went on and as I felt more and more on top of the project I became more and more confident and positive. 'I'm killing this.' As that ratio became overly skewed towards the positive side, pride took over as my positivity moved from functional to destructive in the form of indulgent, delusional joy. I started to think I was bullet proof.

Then came crunch time as our client wheeled out his big guns and I was left feeling severely exposed. In the space of that single meeting my emotions shifted from destructively positive to destructively negative. Briefly, it was what I like to call a 'pity party' as I felt the world collapsing around me. That quickly turned to dread verging on panic as the thought of losing the project took hold.

With my mentor's counsel I was able to regroup. My 'Failure is not an option' belief, underpinned by that inherent confidence, brought me back into the region of functional positivity, initially as calm and then into greater determination, again tempered by trepidation until the point that the project was well and truly back on track.

This framework can be a useful guide to all of us as we face the challenges of our lives. I suspect that few people would argue against the benefits of positivity – 'Think positive' has been a coach's catchcry for generations. Less intuitive is the idea that you can have too much of a good thing, that positivity isn't always functional and can in fact be destructive. Similarly, while we can all understand the detrimental aspects of negative emotional responses like phobias, anxiety, panic, rage and depression, we can overlook the notion that negative emotions can be healthy: flatness after an important presentation can motivate a greater effort ahead of the next one; anger at an injustice can provide the energy to pursue a remedy; trepidation can encourage clear-headed caution.

On a day-to-day basis this framework provides a 'language' against which our emotions can be assessed as to whether they are functional and productive or dysfunctional and destructive; whether they are they helping us have a positive effect on others or they are contributing to a negative effect. This provides a boost to consciousness: you will be more aware of what is going on around you, and better prepared to deal with situations as they arise, or even before they arise. I have little doubt that with greater consciousness on this level at the time of that logistics project, I could well have identified my over-confidence early enough to avoid the client's wrath.

On the other hand, awareness of the different forms that negative thoughts and emotions can take can help us recognise that they are not all destructive, which can be an important component of authentically interacting with our world. Emotions that we can diagnose as being functional – whether positive or negative – are a result of us living by our values, whereas dysfunctional emotions follow when we forget our values and indulge in lower-consciousness behaviour.

Energy as an enabler

Soon after Peta and I moved to Melbourne for me to take up the KPMG position, Peta discovered she was pregnant with our first child. Joshua was born later in 1996, by which time I was fully embedded in my consultancy role, with its relentless workload. I wrapped myself in the pace of the job and became entirely focused on it. I pedalled hard, and when something went wrong I pedalled harder still. Success was all that mattered.

Peta returned to work when Josh was about a year old. As is often the way with these things, my work always came first: if something was wrong with Josh, the phone call would go to Peta. She recalls on more than one occasion driving past my office on her way home to attend to some issue or other, which she did find annoying and somewhat frustrating.

While my hours at work weren't always ridiculous, when I wasn't on the job I was thinking about the job. And I travelled a lot. When our second son, Llewellyn, arrived six weeks early in 1998, I was in the USA. The trouble was that due to a change in itinerary, Peta didn't know exactly where in the US I was at the time. Being before the days of instant, anywhere communication, she ended up using a combination of my mother's knowledge (she knew of family I had been visiting) and her own boss at Qantas to track me down. Her boss managed to identify a flight I was on and had me paged as we disembarked in Pittsburgh. Unfortunately I didn't hear the page. Finally, when I got to my hotel, there was a message from my mother telling me to ring home. As it turned out there were just minutes to spare for me to be able to guide Peta's breathing over the phone! I got home two days after the birth, on Mothers' Day. Needless to say, my absence at Llewellyn's birth is the stuff of regular family recounting.

With two young children, Peta's life now got a lot busier; mine, with work the priority, more or less continued unchanged.

There was no let up once we finally completed the transport company project. The ultimate success of that project saw me promoted very quickly into the role of associate director – a position one level below director in the firm. It was very rare for someone so young and new to the organisation to be moved to this level so rapidly. But, as I mentioned before, the demand for KPMG's services at the time was such that these opportunities were available, and to my partner and her colleagues I had proven my ability. So my honeymoon continued. My ego was well massaged by the idea of being an associate director with this big-four consulting group, and was boosted further by the envious looks of some of my former RAAF colleagues, some of whom had outranked me but were now being left behind. In return for the confidence shown by KPMG, I continued to be fully and constantly engaged in my work and with the travel that went along with it, with my old friends perfectionism, over-caring and stress – along with pumped-up (but mostly functional) positivity – coming along for the ride.

All this had to have some effect on my health. One sign was that I would get sick as soon as I took a holiday. The sudden reduction in adrenaline would expose my immune system and I would catch anything that was going around. Another symptom was bouts of anger or grumpiness at home, waking at three in the morning with my mind racing, and falling asleep on the couch at odd hours. I must have been very hard to live with. My fitness also declined. In the Air Force fitness was a given: we had constant access to good equipment and were expected to pass fitness tests at regular intervals; without that imposed discipline I simply didn't do any regular exercise.

It is blatantly obvious in hindsight that operating at constant full throttle was not the way to get the best out of myself. It makes intuitive sense that investment in your own energy is essential to maintaining optimum performance. Energy in this context is much more than physical fitness. It includes getting sufficient sleep of good quality, eating (and drinking) well, and maintaining your mind through relaxation and genuine (mind switched off) time away from work on weekends and holidays and even in evenings.

Of course, as anyone who has worked in a high-pressure job knows, there can be a chasm between theory and practice in this area. It is just too easy to become so fully absorbed in your work that everything else falls by the wayside. It can be a challenge just to consider doing something about sustaining your physical and mental energy, let alone taking action to achieve this.

The typical 'solution' offered to this challenge is work-life balance. Unfortunately this is not the answer. Work-life balance is a construct that breeds guilt, inadequacy and feelings of failure amongst those who simply can't achieve the sorts of strict separation of work and 'life' that is normally counselled. In the upper echelons of corporate life all that can be achieved by trying to pursue the perfect split is unhappiness at home ('I should be spending more time here') and at work ('I dropped the ball on this by not being here') with a constant sense of being pulled between the two. There is no room for personal space in this scenario, and it is this space that is most critical to the provision of quality input into both your work and home life.

If we focus our priorities on sustaining energy, rather than achieving some arbitrary separation of time, there is much greater potential to operate at an optimum level in all aspects of life.

Sustaining energy can enable growth in consciousness; failing to do so is a powerful blocker of such growth.

We already manage other aspects of our lives when we give them sufficient priority, such as maintenance of our personal hygiene. We (forgive me if I'm generalising) shower, put on clean clothes and brush our teeth as part of our daily routines. Even the busiest amongst us do these things. The trick is to include energy building into our routine in the same way.

Imagine your day as a garage with the capacity to hold 24 hours. Install, say, eight hours sleep and thirty minutes of personal hygiene. What you have remaining is fifteen hours and thirty minutes of space. The question then becomes what you will do with that space or, more importantly, who you will allow to fill it. What most people do is allow others to fill the rest of the garage for them, responding to work demands and family demands first, then any backlog in those two areas if there is any room left. Then they stand back and realise that the garage is full and there's no room left for exercise or any other personal, energy-giving activity. This is exactly what I was doing right through my time at KPMG and beyond.

Today I take a different approach. Now I determine that, each day, I will install in my garage what I need in order to sustain my physical and emotional energy. This includes doing physical exercise as soon as I get up, including aerobic work, resistance work and stretching. This is followed by meditation before a substantial breakfast. By doing these things first, I have effectively put what I need in the garage before anyone or anything else gets a look in, recharged my energy levels and set myself up for the day ahead. To switch analogies, I have 'put my own mask on before that of my child'. What happens next – who fills the remaining time in my daily garage – is now of much less concern than it was before.

How and when you choose to fill your garage is obviously a personal choice. My approach is to claim my own time early in the day so that it cannot be purloined by others under any circumstances. However, you may wish to include time for playing music, or reading to young children, or any of countless other activities that can rejuvenate the soul. Just be aware that leaving your personal 'garage' time until the end of the day greatly increases the chance that you'll find someone has already taken up the space by the time you open the door.

Now, you may feel that I am being unrealistic here. That in the cut and thrust of getting the job done, there just isn't time for an energy recharge. I fully understand this thinking – it was exactly where I was at KPMG. But let's analyse this a little. Think about what is really driving your early rise, answering of emails at five in the morning, scoffing of breakfast, heading into the office for another fast-paced, non-stop day and, finally, late-evening retirement. What's normally behind all that is stress, and behind that again is, if we're honest, a fabricated future of the type I discussed earlier. We pedal harder and harder in our work because that's the only way we see to insure ourselves against a potential disaster: a future in which our world will collapse as our deals don't get done, our monthly figures don't get made, our clients all desert us.

Really?

Do you really think that the sky will fall because you take thirty minutes out of your day for a blood-pumping bike ride each morning? Or because you disappear at lunchtime for a fifteen-minute walk around the block? Or because you spend twenty minutes before going to bed listening to some of your favourite music? Would the outcome of my major project, ultimately leading to promotion and a heightened reputation, have been any different if I'd done any of these things? With the benefit of distance it's very hard to believe that it would have. In fact, with a clearer mind and more energy there's every chance I would have handled the project more efficiently than I did. What was missing for me – and what is missing for many in similar situations – is recognition of the value of maintaining energy levels and/or a solid commitment to reserving time in the day (space in the personal 'garage') for energy maintenance.

There is one other point worth making on this topic before we move on, and that relates to the leadership and organisational implications of energy management. If you are in some sort of leadership position, it is worth asking yourself what you are doing to create an environment in which people feel they have permission to build their energy levels. There are certainly some environments where any time spent 'off the job' is frowned upon. There are others where energy maintenance is actively encouraged. The KPMG environment probably fell somewhere in between: I was given my role on the basis of being driven and self-actualised. It was expected, therefore, that I would know how to look after myself. My heavy workload and failure to look after myself were purely the result of the choices I made – no one else's. Which way you go probably depends on your situation and that of the people working for you. Suffice to say that energy management should be something everyone should be thinking about, and not just from their own, individual, point of view.

Letting go of the control obsession

I spent four years with KPMG before making the decision to shift out of consulting and into the mainstream of corporate life, ultimately taking on a role with Heinz in 1999.

My time with KPMG was, as I mentioned earlier, like one long honeymoon period. I felt on top of the world for almost the whole time. The impetus to look elsewhere came from a combination of factors. One was recognition that having been made an associate director my only next step was partnership, and I wasn't sure that I wanted to enter that world. Another was that the focus of our work started to shift away from re-engineering, which I really enjoyed, towards supply-chain management, which I found less strategic and so less interesting. The buzz started to die down. A third was that I was keen to get some first-hand industry experience – something I had missed out on so far, having moved from the Air Force directly to the consultancy firm.

The position I took up at Heinz was in an advisory capacity to the CEO. It came with the complication that it was based in the regional headquarters in Auckland, a factor made greater by the fact that Peta was pregnant with our third child while our first two kids were still under three. For ten months I commuted between Melbourne and Auckland on a weekly basis. At least for Claire's delivery (as opposed to Llewellyn's) I was in the same country to take Peta to the hospital, though Peta will remind me that that was only because we were able to plan it that way: as doctors decided that Claire's would be a Caesarian birth, we were able to choose a date range based on when I would be at home. Peta and baby Claire also left hospital early, as I had to return to New Zealand. (Another sign of work imposing on our lives is the fact that at the time of Claire's birth, for work reasons I was a resident of New Zealand, so her birth certificate shows her parents as living in different countries!). Later, Peta and the children moved to New Zealand, though we were there only twelve months before the Australasian head office of Heinz was returned to its original location in Melbourne. Back we all came.

My move to Heinz came at an interesting time, as the Australasian business was in the midst of a major restructure. A merger with New Zealand food company Watties was underway, with most production volumes being shifted out of Australia to the Hawkes Bay area on the east coast of New Zealand's North Island. In line with a global rationalisation being driven out of the Heinz headquarters in Pittsburgh, ten of the sixteen combined manufacturing facilities of Heinz and Watties across Australasia were being closed, new information technology systems were being implemented and substantial rebranding was taking place. All of this was being overseen by the CEO, a leader with enormous energy, a relentless work ethic, a highly strategic mind and a deep knowledge of business. For me the learning curve was steep. Although my role was essentially that of a consultant, something I now had some solid background in, the dynamics of internal consultancy were quite different. I had not in the past been exposed to the groove of day-to-day 'business as usual' in which a corporate firm operates – as an external consultant at KPMG this was not something that ever really concerned us.

Looking back, one of the things I accomplished best at Heinz was to manage the control I had over the job.

The subject of control in our working lives is something that most of us have to grapple with in one way or another, often at many times and in many different situations.

If there is a standard template for the notion of control in one's career it is this: We start in junior roles with little direct control over our time (i.e. we essentially react to whatever it is that the boss wants done) or over our organisation (i.e. our own actions are unlikely to have a significant impact on the direction of the organisation). As we move up the ranks and gain experience and knowledge, we gain more control over our time (we increasingly have the power to use our time as we see fit, provided we get the job done) and the organisation (the more senior we are the more we can steer the organisation, and those in it, in the direction we see fit). Reaching the 'ultimate' role of, say, CEO, is to be captain of the ship with overarching authority.

This is the trajectory many of us think our careers will take. We see the attainment of increased control over time as something to strive for, while the extent to which we succeed in achieving a level of control in the organisations we work for will be rewarded with promotions.

Of course in practice this is largely a furphy. In reality, climbing up the hierarchy takes many of us into middle management, where we find ourselves squeezed by the demands of both sides: those working for us and those we work for. There is very little control of time in this situation, while control of the organisation is notional at best. Here we start to learn how difficult it is to translate rank into results via the efforts of others. Make it to the top and not a lot changes. As Neville, my first CEO at Heinz, puts it: 'Being a person who leads the organisation is sometimes more helpless than people who are direct cogs on the wheel … you think you are the big cog but eventually realise that you are quite limited in your ability to get others to do what you think is the right thing'.

My career did not follow this standard path. As a result, along the way I had the benefit of learning some different lessons about the realities of control. While an obsession with control was not the most powerful aspect of my ego, I have been able to progressively cede control in many situations over the last fifteen years or so.

Aside from the relatively stringent control imposed on us as ADFA cadets, my first real exposure to the challenges of control was as a junior officer at Amberley. You will recall my being dropped in, as a very young ADFA graduate, to lead a unit that included some troops with very substantial service under their belts. Control? I'd say mine at this point was close to zero – perhaps marginally above simply because I had a stripe on my shoulder. I had much more control when the commercialisation project came along – we were all on a par experience wise at the start of that, so my leadership was more readily deferred to. My sense of control was diminished again when I moved to KPMG, particularly on that early transport assignment involving the five-in-the-morning meeting in Sydney. Control in the major logistics assignment initially felt greater by virtue of the fact that I had direct access to the senior people in the organisation, including the CEO; the run-in with the internal sponsor shattered that sense of control, the realisation coming that while I had access to these senior people, as a consultant I was still an outsider.

Today I have a more pragmatic understanding of the nature of control. It was something I garnered largely through my KPMG experience and nurtured at Heinz. Instrumental to this was some fantastic insight and experience of control in the context of a facilitation environment. That insight has proven to be applicable in a much broader range of scenarios than just facilitation.

Early in my time at KPMG, my managing partner pulled me aside after a workshop I had facilitated. The workshop didn't quite get the result we were looking for and I was left a bit rattled.

'What you did,' she told me, 'was you worked out what you were trying to achieve with that group, then you worked out the exact pathway you would have the group follow in order to get to that end result. The problem came when, for various reasons, the workshop deviated away from your planned pathway. At that point it all went a bit haywire.'

She was dead right. I did have a precise plan for the workshop laid out. With my perfectionism firmly strapped on (along with over-caring, I suspect, in wanting to appear on top of things to the participants), I had spent a long time preparing for the workshop and mapping out my intended path.

The partner's advice was to maintain a clear focus on the desired outcome. 'Beyond that, be flexible and allow the workshop to take any of the hundred or more potential routes to that final result.'

I spent quite a bit of time with my KPMG mentor after that. He was a master of what was called 'freedom within a framework': the art of keeping your eye on the prize while allowing great flexibility in how it is won. I had actually seen him do this back on the RAAF project but hadn't appreciated his skill. With his mentoring, I started to realise what a master of 'working the room' he was as a facilitator. He provided me with enormous assistance as I slowly built up my own ability to facilitate in this way. Today, 'facilitation without a safety net', or 'empathy-based facilitation', not only guides my approach to facilitation but also to building influence inside organisations.

Today my approach to control is guided by a simple but powerful principle: Focus on the things you can control at the absolute exclusion of those that you cannot. Understanding and working with this principle is fundamental to resilience; fighting against it – constantly striving to control that which you have no control over – leads only to distress and endless frustration.

By the time I got to Heinz I was more comfortable with this

principle myself. I needed to be, because as an advisor to the CEO without direct line responsibilities – essentially an internal consultant – there was a lot I could not directly control. My role was largely in strategy and project development; to gain buy-in to this I needed to build good working relationships with a wide range of people across the business. A lot of my time, therefore, was spent listening, trying to understand the issues facing individuals and identifying those who did have the control. The CEO, who was watching me do this, describes what I did as 'broadening [my] connections … less reliant on hierarchy, those above and below, but rather working upstream and downstream [of processes]'. In summary, my aim was not to try and exert control by pulling rank – I knew from past experience that even in the defence force that doesn't work. Instead, as the CEO described, I invested my efforts in building influence with those who did have the control.

This is perhaps the most significant lesson I have learnt about control: that regardless of your formal scope of control, your actual scope lies in your ability to build relationships and influence others toward a mutually attractive goal.

There was one aspect of the Heinz job in which I did have a lot of control compared with what I'd had in the past: time. Inside work, the pressure and demands on my time, while high, were not at the level they had been at KPMG. Outside work, at least in that first period, I was living away from my family. I was staying in a bed and breakfast in one of Auckland's hippest areas, surrounded by some of the city's best restaurants. Enough said! In a way I ended up with too much time – too much control? – and this in itself became a challenge. This is not to say that I was sitting around twiddling my thumbs, but I was less time pressured than I had been in the past.

By 2001 I was becoming disenchanted with the role at Heinz. Various factors came into play. The influence of the global head office, and particularly the removal of the CEO at short notice after a period of poor financial results, was an ugly side of control as applied from a distance. My role, while challenging at times (and I did eventually take on leadership roles in sales and then supply chain), became more routine, settling into a cycle of business as usual, regular reporting and strategic planning. And I had worked out that climbing the corporate ladder – the pursuit of ever greater control – was not for me. I enrolled in a Masters of Finance degree course, thinking that my future might lie back in some form of consulting around financial strategies, perhaps in mergers and acquisitions. In retrospect this was a good example of the 'Energy is king' principle inverted: my energy level was depleting not because of overwork and lack of care for myself, but because of a lack of challenge, a lack of pressure. To reprise the pressure-performance curve introduced in Chapter 1, I was now operating well down the 'comfort' part of the curve.

All in all, by the middle of 2001 I was becoming decidedly itchy. However, as is often the nature of corporate life, even when the intellectual challenge is diminished, my days were flat out and I didn't get around to seriously looking for something else. Nor did I get around to going to the doctor when, in November, I started getting very strong pains in my head whenever I blew my nose.

I should have.

Assertive Humility

CHAPTER 4

Cancer: the bandana

Assertive Humility

After all the travel of recent years – not just my own but by Peta's
and the kids' as well – Christmas in 2001 was a bit different. For
once we didn't travel to family interstate, but rather celebrated
at our home in Melbourne. This had given us the chance to buy a
swing set for our kids (two, three and five years old at the time),
which I assembled on Christmas Eve in the backyard, with a couple
of mates. A spanner in one hand and a beer in the other – what
better way to spend the night before Christmas? Life was good.

The pain associated with blowing my nose showed no signs of
abating by the end of December, and if anything, was getting worse.
It was very intense: a strong, heavy ache starting at my forehead
then radiating through the rest of my head. It was excruciating, at
times causing me to fall to my knees.

I finally made an appointment to see a doctor in early January, just
after going back to work. Though I didn't suspect it at the time, I
was about to change my hat again. This time I would be swapping
my corporate hat for something entirely different – a bandana.

The doctor diagnosed a sinus infection and gave me a prescription
for antibiotics. Somehow I just had a feeling that this wasn't right,
that there was more to it than a simple infection, and I pushed him
to send me for a scan. He obliged, and a couple of days later I went
off for a CT scan. After the scan the radiographer gave me a sealed
envelope containing the scan and report, which he asked me to let
my GP open so the results could be discussed with me.

Assertive Humility

In a sign that I had well and truly outgrown the 'rule taker' nature of my youth – I would never have ignored a request like that at school – I opened the envelope as soon as I got to the car. I didn't expect a bad report – I didn't get bad reports – but I did want to know what was in there. Of course, I could hardly understand anything in the report, couched as it was in the secret language used by medical practitioners to communicate with each other, so I went home and used the internet to help me crack the code. The main word on the report was 'glioma', which I discovered is a form of brain tumour. That didn't sound good. Still, neither Peta nor I have any medical background so, while we were undoubtedly concerned, I think deep down we still imagined that this wouldn't amount to much. After all, we were a young, healthy couple with small children: bad things didn't happen to us – they happened to other people.

When we went to the see my doctor the next day he confirmed what I had learned myself and made clear the potential for the tumour to be cancerous. Now the dread started to grow, though still we suppressed it. To an external observer Peta and I would have appeared quite clinical about the whole thing. In truth, I didn't want to panic Peta, and she didn't want to put undue stress on me – it was a case of mutually assured detachment. I continued to work, Peta continued to manage the house and kids ahead of returning to work for the new year herself. It will be alright, we told ourselves. A second, finer, CT scan was ordered, though it didn't do much more than confirm the presence of the glioma. This was followed by an MRI.

The MRI made denial much more difficult. It clearly showed the presence of a golf-ball-sized tumour at the front of the left frontal lobe of my brain – at the top of my forehead at the hairline, just above my left eye. The MRI also provided more detail. It confirmed the glioma as most likely a so-called grade 3 anaplastic astrocytoma. Malignancy in a tumour of this kind was not just possible, it was highly likely – and if that was the case the prognosis was extremely dire. Combined with the increasingly severe symptoms I was experiencing (with more frequent and severe headaches), the recommendation was that surgery – brain surgery – to remove the tumour be undertaken as soon as possible. Surgery would also allow categorical confirmation of whether or not the glioma was cancerous.

In reading more about malignant anaplastic astrocytoma, one thing stood out above all others: a typical life expectancy of no more than two and a half years.

Things were serious now. Both Peta and I understood this. I was only thirty-two years old, yet death was already appearing on my horizon. Still, even with this prospect, and countless other questions and 'what-ifs' swirling around our minds, we still managed to maintain a degree of emotional detachment. By now, though, it was time that we broke the news to family and friends.

In a way, sharing the situation with our families was made easier by their all living interstate. I rang my brother and sister, who were both still living in Inverell. It was organised that they would be with our mum, Dorothy, when I called to tell her. The call wasn't very long and the job was done; obviously there was shock, but distance couldn't help but numb the emotions at both ends of the line. I would later learn that it was after this call that my family decided to take action on selling the family business, something they had been thinking about for some time.

Telling Peta's mum, Carol, was also daunting, given she had not only lost her husband at a young age but also been left with very young children at the time. However, Carol is very practical and her first thoughts turned to how she could support Peta and me through the surgery and beyond.

The toughest of these conversations was with a close friend – someone we had met through a mothers' group after our first child, Josh, was born. Having lost her own husband to a brain tumour while pregnant with her first child, this friend knew better than almost anyone else what we were going through, and would be going through. On first hearing the news she thought I was joking – she told me off for being so black. As reality sank in, her face dissolved and she responded with an explosion of grief. Her reaction broke something inside Peta and me and we finally allowed the gravity of our situation to surface. The rational, clinical poise we had succeeded in maintaining to this point was shattered, both of us allowing tears, anger and frustration to show.

Then there was advising my boss and colleagues at Heinz, and so many other people in our lives. I think one of the most challenging aspects of a situation like this – particularly for someone like me who was used to being fairly private and reserved on personal matters – is having to explain your situation, and answer questions about it, over and over again.

It came as a surprise to me that I had to choose my own neurosurgeon. It's not quite like choosing a hairdresser, where you can just let any mistakes grow out if you're not happy. It's certainly not an easy thing to do when you have little in the way of medical knowledge and no real criteria against which to make a reasoned decision. Somehow I found it within myself to put aside my need for perfectionism – in a black sort of way the process ended up being almost comical, with humour forming part of the selection process for us. At this point I might let Peta tell the story as she remembers it best:

On meeting with the first neurosurgeon Stuart was asked a lot of questions, one of which was which hand he writes with. Stuart replied that he uses his left. The doctor asked if he also plays sport left-handed, to which Stuart replied no – 'I play golf, tennis and so on right-handed'. To be certain this was important in ascertaining the potential impact of removing the tumour – the doctor asked Stuart to confirm that he plays all sport right-handed, to which Stuart replied that no, 'I swim with both hands'. This response was met deadpan by the surgeon. Later, when discussing possible cognitive impairment, Stuart asked whether he would be able to do cryptic crosswords after surgery. When the doctor assured him that he would, all going well, Stuart replied, 'That's great, because I sure as hell can't do them now'. Again a deadpan response. This lack of any interaction ultimately put Stuart off this surgeon.

The second neurosurgeon had more interpersonal skills. He presented Stuart with two options – a biopsy or a wait-and-see approach – given that the glioma had still not been confirmed as cancerous. Stuart really did not like either option, though ultimately the thought of a foreign mass in his head that could be malignant did not sit well with him, so the wait-and-see approach was not going to get off the ground.

The final surgeon Stuart 'interviewed', and the one he ultimately chose, was young and seemed approachable. He also had small hands, which was somehow appealing – Stuart did not want a doctor with huge hands to be messing around in his head. Later we found out that at the time of the surgery, the neurosurgeon had only just become a father for the first time, to which Stuart responded, 'Well you would not have got the job had I realised you were going to be sleep deprived, small hands or not'.

I went into hospital on the 23rd of January, barely a fortnight after my first visit to the doctor, for surgery the next day. By now my whole family had come down from Inverell and Peta's mother, Carol, had travelled from the Gold Coast. I remember everyone gathered around my bed. At one point a nurse offered to put on a video explaining a craniotomy, the surgery I was having. I was initially keen, but after seeing the look of horror on my mum's face, I declined.

On the morning of the operation my head was shaved and 'marked up' with all the surgery plans. My pulse raced. There were so many possible consequences: I might have a stroke with various forms of potential residual damage; I might lose a degree of cognitive function; I might lose the ability to speak.

I might die.

Even though I knew I was in good hands and had done enough research of my own to know that the chances of survival, at the very least, were positive, I still felt a heavy nervousness as I was wheeled to the theatre. I can't begin to know what it was like for Peta, who walked beside me – I still feel emotional writing this sentence now.

Of course the surgery was relatively easy for me. Once in theatre, an anaesthetic was administered and I was unconscious in seconds. It was my family, left to wait for three hours, pushing food around their plates at a nearby restaurant and making small talk, who were struggling now. Peta talks about how she found herself bargaining with God:

> *At a pre-surgery meeting, our surgeon had outlined the risks associated with the surgery. The worst outcome would be that Stuart would die during surgery. Please God do not let this happen. There was no default position on this option. Please God let him live. There was also a possibility that he could have a stroke, leaving him with residual damage, the precise nature of which we would not know until after the surgery. Please God do not let this happen. If you let him live, can you please let him not have a stroke. Another complication could be that he lost cognitive function, exactly what and to what degree we did not know. Please God do not let this happen. If you let him live and he doesn't have a stroke can he please keep his cognitive function. There was a risk that Stuart's speech – more particularly speech production – might be*

affected by a condition with which you know what you want to say but are unable to produce the words. Please God do not let this happen. If you let him live, and he doesn't have a stroke, and he has all his cognitive function, can he please have his speech. I was obviously working on the worst-case scenario first. Really I just wanted him alive and if this was achieved I worked down my list of scenarios from the worst to the least bad. Let's face it, none of them were good. I must have gone through this dozens of times while Stuart was in surgery. Please God make him well.

The family's wait finally ended with good news. When I eventually came out of unconsciousness I learnt that the tumour had been successfully and completely, they felt, removed. Scans soon afterwards showed no signs of remaining cancerous material. And despite the thirty-two staples holding my skull together I was able to play – and win – Scrabble against my siblings, much to their chagrin. They had seen an opportunity to beat me for once, but my cognitive ability had clearly come through unscathed.

However, we still had the pathology test results to get through. Told they could take up to ten days, we were surprised when our surgeon asked to see Peta and me privately after only two or three. The news wasn't good. He then told us that my tumour had been confirmed as a malignant, grade 3, anaplastic astrocytoma – a tumour characterised by fast, aggressive growth, and invasion of neighbouring tissue. The surrounding tissue would need to be attacked with intensive radiotherapy in order to try and kill off any remaining cancer cells, but the chances of success were not high.

Damien was reticent to lock in a number relating to my prognosis, but when pressed eventually confirmed what we had read: that the typical life expectancy of sufferers of this tumour is about two and a half years.

We were back to square one. Our immediate reaction was tears and a sense of defeat, both trying to console each other. Really at no point prior to this had the concept of death seemed so real. I remained completely melancholic for at least a week and relapsed into it for some time afterwards. I would wake up in the middle of the night crying – something I had never done before. However, with the encouragement of my family – I still remember Peta's mother saying, 'At least it's not a grade 4 – you can beat this!' – I found myself again able to focus on the future, at least the near term. Peta, on the other hand (and I didn't know this until much later) was torn between trying to stay positive and planning for a future in which all the indications were that she was going to lose me. She describes thinking about the songs that she would have played at my funeral; wondering whether or not the kids, still under five, should attend the funeral; would she move back to the Gold Coast or stay in Melbourne?

Optimism as an enabler

It's probably a good time to revisit the earlier discussion about positivity, as the situation Peta and I found ourselves in now was clearly going to test Fredrickson's ideal 2.9:1 positive to negative ratio.

Assertive Humility

As we have seen, positivity had been a fairly strong feature of
my life up to the point of my diagnosis – sometimes beneficially,
sometimes not (when, as in that logistics project hiccup, I allowed
my positivity to become delusional). But it's fair to say that none
of the challenges I had faced so far was on the same scale as the
cancer. More seriously – and I was not aware of this at the time
– the way in which I chose to see my situation cognitively was
probably going to have some impact on my chances of recovery.

Volumes have been written about the psychology of optimism and
its stablemate, pessimism.

Psychologists have recognised for some time that whether one takes
an optimistic or pessimistic view of challenging situations is not
'hard wired', but is rather a matter of the way you choose to see
those events[1]. In other words, as Martin Seligman wrote, optimism
can be learned.

Also well understood is the notion that optimism and pessimism
can operate on different levels in line with those of positivity and
negativity. So there is a difference between 'realistic optimism',
in which you believe you can succeed with the right effort, and
'Pollyanna optimism', which is essentially blind faith that success
will just come. Similarly, there is a difference between 'pragmatic
pessimism' ('There's a good chance I'll fail if I don't act, so I'd better
understand what could go wrong') and 'melancholy pessimism'
('Woe is me – I'm stuffed').

[1] Recall the earlier reference to Albert Ellis and his ABC model.

Figure 5 is the way I like to represent the relationship between these levels in my work.

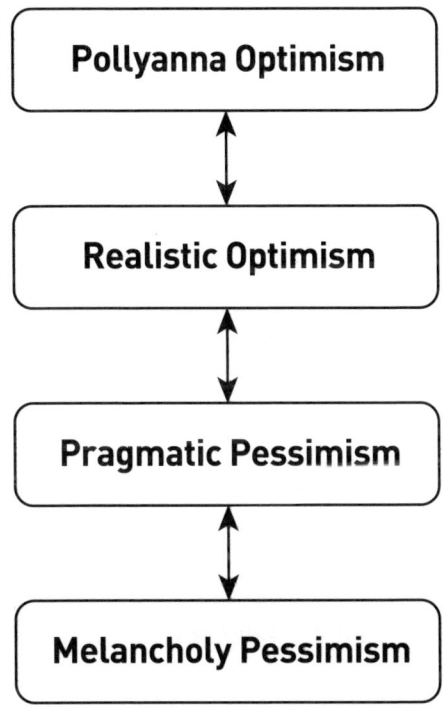

Figure 5: Levels of optimism and pessimism

Looking back now, I understand that while, at a given level of consciousness, we may have a tendency towards one of these four levels of outlook, immediate circumstances can see us swing between different levels quite quickly.

Up to the point of diagnosis I would say my outlook about most things was generally realistic optimism, bordering on occasion with pragmatic pessimism. As a qualified engineer, the latter was really where I belonged: engineers are trained to look for all the ways in which a design might fail, which is classic pragmatic pessimism. It was probably pragmatic pessimism that prompted me to push my doctor to send me for a CT scan, rather than accepting his initial diagnosis of sinusitis.

Peta's and my initial reaction to the results of my scans – disbelief with a degree of almost clinical emotional detachment – was certainly closer to Pollyanna optimism. I would imagine this is where most people start a cancer journey, before the realities of a possible bleak future hit home. For us that happened when breaking the news to family and, especially, friends, which saw us rapidly, albeit briefly, move into melancholy pessimism. To this day Peta believes this was the most traumatic aspect of the whole experience.

There were so many questions in my mind in these early days, few of which could ever be answered. To this day I wonder whether the stress caused by my perfectionist/over-caring personality over many years could have contributed to my illness. Whether my failure to attend to my health and energy during my corporate career made a difference. Even whether years of having a mobile phone practically attached to my ear could have been a factor. There was certainly plenty of scope for 'what if' questioning and fabricating of very dire futures.

I'm sure there must have been moments of 'Life isn't fair' thinking through this period also, though, as I mentioned earlier, the death of my father had shaken most of that out of me. It was our general positivity that saw Peta and me move quite quickly out of melancholy pessimism and back into pragmatic pessimism.

I did an enormous amount of data gathering and internet research after my diagnosis, trying to understand what my prognosis was, what the best and worst outcomes might be, what the statistics were around each of these and everything in between. By the time we met potential neurosurgeons, I had crawled my way back to a point of realistic optimism. 'We will get through this. What can we do to maximise our chances of doing so?' Despite the nervousness before (and, for Peta, during) the surgery, its positive result meant we came out the other side of that with the realistic optimism still in place. In brief moments of euphoria, given how dire the outcome might have been, we perhaps even allowed ourselves a bit of Pollyanna optimism at this stage. Things were looking up.

Then, of course, the confirmation of cancer knocked us straight down again. My prognosis was so grim – so close to the worst-case scenarios we had been reading about – that in the immediate aftermath melancholy pessimism seemed the only place to be. But, once again, with the support of each other plus family and friends, we lifted ourselves out of this state and back into pragmatic pessimism. In six weeks, after my scar had healed, I would be facing radiotherapy – that gave me something new to research and understand. For Peta, a level of pragmatism, including thinking about those questions around funeral preparation, was the only option. As she describes it, planning for the future, for your own survival come what may, is essential. And, practically speaking, should I have died the world was not going to stop for her or the children – they would have to keep moving forward and she needed to be prepared for that. But this pragmatism came with the price of an enormous and unceasing sense of guilt on Peta's behalf. Every thought that acknowledged the possibility of my not being around felt like treachery to her; like giving up. She remembers the worst of these thoughts being almost resignation to the unwavering certainty that I would die – thoughts she obviously kept to herself at the time. This push and pull, towards wanting to be optimistic but needing to be practical, is realistic optimism at its strongest.

Cancer stirs up a broader and more dramatic range of responses from sufferers, and those close to them, than perhaps any other disease. The regular portrayal of cancer in fiction may contribute to this, or the fact that cancer is so common that few remain completely untouched by it. Whatever the cause, the whole gamut of the optimism/pessimism spectrum is well covered by those with cancer. Most of us have heard stories of those at one end of the scale who seem to yield to cancer, never able to get above melancholic pessimism. Then there are those at the other end, the Pollyanna optimists, who believe that 'believing' is all they need to do to survive. In between are those who tend towards realistic optimism or pragmatic pessimism, as I've discussed. In all four groups you will find examples of survivors and those who don't make it: cancer is simply too complex for survival to depend solely on mindset, though my view today is that mindset can certainly play a role.

I also believe that mindset, in terms of where one sits on the pessimism/optimism scale, can have an impact on business and career. Charging ahead with Pollyanna optimism can blind you to warning signs of trouble ahead. Similarly, wallowing in melancholy pessimism when something goes wrong can cause you to overlook potential ways out, as well as infecting others and spreading the thinking style; melancholy pessimism is contagious. Both of these mindsets might be described as having a 'closed-eye' approach to the future. By contrast, realistic optimism is more robust, more resilient. It is more open to possibility and uncertainty, characterised by a greater willingness to change direction if necessary. It acknowledges that there is rarely just one path between where you are now and where you want to get to.

If you detect in this last discussion a 'greyer' – that is, less black and white – view of the world than was my style through Cub, RAAF and corporate hat-wearing years, you would be right. It is a shift that arguably started on the day my tumour was discovered, but which was given a significant boost by ten days I would spend on a cancer retreat. The retreat, and my health circumstances going into it, would open my mind to a more spiritual outlook on life and catalyse a significant shift in thinking as a bandana became my hat of choice.

It was my sister, Janine – a naturopath and always the more spiritual member of the family – who suggested I consider booking into the Gawler Foundation program, run by Ian Gawler, after my surgery. The ten-day, live-in retreat would cover a range of issues – everything from diet to meditation to coming to terms with death. I was dubious, as it all sounded at odds with my very rational view of the world, but with the encouragement of Peta and Janine I eventually signed up to attend a program in early March of 2002, before the start of my radiotherapy.

One of the most profound experiences of the retreat came right at the start. Walking into the workshop room, I was surrounded by thirty-five sick people, many wearing bandanas. Many of them looked quite poorly. It was only then that I realised that I was one of these people – that to any outsider I would have been seen as an equal member of this group, a cancer sufferer. I was sick too.

The program included a number of sessions that challenged my typical ways of thinking, encouraging me to open my mind and discover a more spiritual side. But it also, to the benefit of rationalists like me, provided a scientific, research-backed justification of practices such as meditation, describing, for instance, the impact of meditation on hormonal balancing of cortisol and serotonin, stimulation of the immune system, pain management and sleep optimisation.

There were one-on-one conversations, in which we would take turns answering, with increasing depth, a question like 'What do you hate most about your cancer?' or 'What is your greatest fear?'.
I found this intensely confronting in the early stages – the first time all I could do was cry. Eventually I was able to start articulating my reality and my fears.

There were long discussions about death and dying. We had all been

asked to read Ian's book, *You can Conquer Cancer,* before the retreat.
When Ian asked how many of us had read it, nearly all the hands
went up. Then he asked how many had read the chapter on death
and dying. Only eight hands were raised. Most of us, including me,
were clearly not willing to square up to that topic.

Four choices

Over the course of a few days at the retreat, one activity involved
spending time working on a series of line drawings on various
themes such as 'a memory of your childhood' and 'something
of your current life'. One day, in preparation for pair coaching,
Ian walked around the room, stopping at most pictures to draw
out some discussion points or provide insight. He reached me,
paused, and kept walking. I couldn't help but feel a little neglected
– momentarily transported back to the over-caring nature of the
primary-school me, perhaps. In the end, though, he called me up
after he had completed his circuit and used me and my work as the
subject of a lengthy coaching session to demonstrate the process
in front of the whole group. I started with another outpouring of
emotion, oblivious to the other members of the group, and became
engulfed in the conversation with Ian.

One of my drawings was of me on a bike path in Melbourne,
alongside a river. Ahead was a fork, with the choice of going over a
bridge or continuing along the river. Ian used the imagery to help
me make conscious, and verbalise, the reality that my cancer had
brought me to a fork like this: I could keep going as I was, or I could

choose a different path. I am convinced that this single conversation was the catalyst for my change in life direction.

Back in Chapter 2 I introduced the subject of beliefs and choices and their role in blocking or enabling the emergence of consciousness. To reiterate, I summarised the belief-centred concept, or understanding of the world, that said:

> *It's not the world that drives my emotions and behaviours, it's what I believe about the world that drives my emotions and behaviours.*

I also introduced Albert Ellis's ABC model, which states that the emotions and behaviours that we display in response to an event (the 'consequences') result from a combination of the event itself and, importantly, the beliefs we bring to the event. Ultimately, we choose our beliefs, and we have the power to change them should we wish to.

All of this is nicely captured in the words of Peta's mum, Carol: 'It's not what happens to you in life; it's how you choose to respond to it'.

The trouble with talking about choice in this way is that it can be overwhelming. In so many aspects of life we seem to be faced with myriad choices. It's bad enough when we go shopping, but when we need to choose an emotional and behavioural response to a situation there would appear to be an infinite number of options.

In reality it is much simpler than this. In every negative situation we encounter – from getting stuck in traffic to being diagnosed with cancer – there are really only four possible choices facing us.

The first choice is to take positive action.

The second choice is do nothing – to accept and make peace with the situation.

The third choice is to do nothing but ruminate with anger, frustration, contempt, sadness, fear, worry, guilt, shame, embarrassment, etc.

The fourth choice is to act destructively.

Choices	Functional	Dysfunctional
Do nothing	**Make Peace** Accept; make peace; let it go	**Ruminate** Get angry, sad, fearful; lay blame (silently)
Take action	**Take Positive Action** Change the environment from 'bad' to 'good'	**Dysfunctional** Lash out, seek retribution, blame (loudly)

Figure 6: Four choices in response to a negative situation

In the context of the drawing I made on the cancer retreat, the third choice equated to ignoring the bridge and staying on my existing path, allowing myself to get angry, cry 'Life's not fair!', and spend whatever time I had left bemoaning what had been and how it had disrupted my life. This choice was never going to be the one I would make. I had already learnt that life isn't always fair, and if I had any doubts I only had to look at my mother, or Carol, or our mothers' group friend – all of whom had lost husbands far too early – for a harsh reminder. What's more, the consciousness raising that had taken place on the retreat had given me a good start in coming to terms with my illness. Anger and self-pity weren't going to achieve anything. Similarly, the fourth choice – negative action – was not a reality either. What was I going to do? Sue my mobile phone company, or my employers, for exposing me to a risk for which there was no conclusive evidence?

Choice number two was to stay on my existing path and calmly accept the consequences. I could take the completely rational, modern medical approach to beating my cancer. Should I win that battle, I could put my illness behind me, rejoin the corporate race and continue as I had been – put the corporate hat back on and continue the 'dash for cash'. This choice was not going to get a look-in either. I simply had too much to live for not to try everything I could. Later, after my radiotherapy and return to work, it would quickly become apparent that staying on my existing path on the work front was not a realistic option either.

The reality was that I had already made the first choice – to cross the bridge and follow a new path – by agreeing to attend the cancer retreat in the first place. Over time, making this choice would mean a wholesale shift in many aspects of my life, from my approach to spirituality to my diet to my work. There would be no turning back. The retreat prised open a crack in my consciousness brought on by the cancer diagnosis, and that crack could only widen.

Initially, making the choice to take positive action meant complementing orthodox medical treatments with so-called alternative approaches. My perfectionism returned, now in a dedication to adopting the dietary principles I had learnt on the retreat, all designed to give my body, and my immune system in particular, the greatest chance of surviving the assault that would come from radiotherapy. With 'military precision', as Peta describes it, I removed alcohol, coffee, all sugars, saturated fats and meat from my diet, replacing them with vegetable juices, herbal teas and organic fruit and vegetables in large quantities.

Over the next year, and beyond that, my choice would lead to further changes, as I will describe in the next chapter.

Of course, the choices I made around my cancer treatment and approach to life thereafter were made over a period of time, with plenty of thinking along the way. But the concept of these four basic choices facing us in any situation remains the same, whether that situation is long term or immediate and short term, and whether that situation is positive or negative.

Caught in traffic, we can get violent (choice 4), honking the horn or even getting out and abusing other drivers through their windows.

We can get angry (choice 3); stressed that we will be late (choice 3); relax and come to terms with the situation, understanding that we can't control other drivers (choice 2); or do something positive: (anything from choose a different route next time to taking political action to force an improvement in the road system (choice 1).

Faced with an employee who isn't pulling their weight, we can angrily sack them (choice 4), be frustrated and treat them with contempt (choice 3), be accepting (choice 2: perhaps they add value in other ways) or take positive action (choice 1: from understanding their reasons, to coaching, up-skilling or performance counselling, to moving them on in an orderly and compassionate fashion).

Dealing with noisy neighbours late at night we can toss, turn and curse in our bed (choice 3) or dig out some earplugs from deep inside the bathroom cupboard (choice 2). We can act functionally (choice 1, via personal intervention or calling in the local constabulary) or dysfunctionally (choice 4, letting down the neighbours' tyres).

You get the idea.

A similar range of choices faces us in a positive situation. On winning the lottery we could act functionally (choice 1), perhaps by investing for the future and making some generous donations; act dysfunctionally (choice 4) by spending the money in haste, or gambling it away; do nothing and change nothing, putting the money aside for a rainy day (choice 2); or do nothing but start worrying about the possibility of being robbed or ripped off and losing it all (choice 3).

It is not that one choice or the other is the 'right' one in any of these situations, nor that one choice or another is going to be right every time. For a start, we need to choose our battles: choosing to take action on every challenge would be to send yourself mad but, equally, allowing yourself to get angry or even violent in response to everything that doesn't go your way would also be health destroying.

Soon after the cancer retreat it was time to approach radiotherapy. While it would seem there was no choice in this matter, in fact there was. There are people who choose to skip radiotherapy, given its side effects, and either pursue alternative approaches or do nothing. But in the spirit of throwing everything possible at my challenge, I went for choice 2 – accept and make peace with the approach. Radiotherapy (sometimes known as radiation therapy) has been used for over 100 years to kill cancer cells. The technology of delivery has evolved enormously over that time, but the basic principle – the draconian blasting of cells with concentrated radiation – is largely unchanged.

As usual I was keen to learn as much as I could before the radiotherapy started. So it was that when Peta and I went to the Peter MacCallum Cancer Centre to meet my oncologist for the first time, I went well armed with peer-reviewed journal articles, statistics on recovery and a lot of questions. That's not to say that I wasn't nervous – just walking into the cancer centre is enough to make you anxious. After all, as Peta puts it, 'This is where the really sick people go – you know, the ones who actually die'. But the oncologist was immensely professional and calm, providing both realistic reassurance and detailed answers to all my questions, and certainly made us feel as comfortable as was possible under the circumstances.

Radiotherapy is, to put it mildly, a form of torture. It started with the creation of a plastic mask – my *Silence of the Lambs* mask: lying on the treatment bench, a heavy sheet of pliable, mesh-like plastic was draped over my head, stretched tight and pinned to the table. The mask then hardened; it would be used to hold my head in precisely the same position during each of my treatments over the coming weeks. Treatments took place over seven weeks, five days a week. I travelled into the centre from home each time, returning exhausted and able to do nothing but sleep.

The importance of team –
and gratitude

Something that made the radiotherapy more bearable was a simple gesture from my second CEO at Heinz. She organised for a company driver to chauffeur me to and from each of my radiotherapy sessions. This made an enormous difference to all of us, but particularly Peta, as she continued to manage our household and three young children.

It was one of countless acts of generosity that we were provided with during and after my cancer treatment, all of which have contributed to my recovery and made life easier in one way or another. They have all given me a heightened appreciation of the importance of 'team', not only in difficult circumstances but also in life in general.

I knew this pre-cancer, of course, but once again I had not appreciated it. I grew up in a small town where community – 'pitching in' – is always important. At ADFA and in the RAAF, team is the only way. During our 'Cryptic Challenge' as second-year cadets, it was the group of us working together that got us over the line. Later, on the Commercial Support Program project with my RAAF unit, it was the team that enabled us to complete our submission on time. At KPMG on the large logistics program it was the team working for me who got the job done, and the support of the team above me that kept me on track when things started going pear shaped. And so on. All of us, if we look closely, have teams around us working collectively to overcome whatever obstacles may fall in our way.

So it was with my cancer, in myriad ways. My family and Peta's, who dropped everything and came to Melbourne soon after I was diagnosed. Carol volunteering to stay home with the kids during my period in hospital during and after surgery, making it much easier for my birth family to support me. A close friend who organised a boys' night out a few nights before my surgery, giving me the chance to relax with a few mates. The school community who provided meals for the family during the toughest period, and who 'blitzed' our backyard with a massive tidy up and transformation. Our neighbour who emptied the high gutters on our house after he noticed them overflowing in the rain; only after finishing the job was it revealed that he didn't even clean his own gutters normally, as he is afraid of heights. Friends and family who went out of their way to accommodate my unusual diet.

We also need to appreciate the wider team we have around us at times – the silent and often faceless people who do team-like things. When, a bit later, I took up swimming to try and regain some fitness, I needed to be monitored due to the risk of seizures (common after brain surgery). Every time, for lap after lap, a lifeguard at our local swimming pool would trace my movements up and down the pool, just in case. And then, of course, there were the countless doctors and nurses for whom I could have been 'just another patient' but was never made to feel that way.

And of course there are those who form our most close-knit team: the partners and carers. It is impossible to measure the extent to which Peta has contributed to my recovery. While dealing with the emotional turbulence of coming to grips with my initial diagnosis and an uncertain future, and all the ups and downs since, Peta also had to continue her day job with Qantas as well as manage the family, including our three then-young children. Any mother knows how busy a 'normal' house is with kids that age. Throw in caring for a husband with a serious illness, emotionally charged trips to doctors, the complexity of shopping for both the family and said husband's intricate (read non-supermarket) diet, and taking on additional tasks like managing the finances … let's just say there wasn't much opportunity in there for Peta to attend to her own energy levels. On top of all that it is the primary carer who ends up acting as communications officer: it was Peta who had to answer endless questions about my welfare, while also absorbing the awkwardness of those who would dance around the subject, or avoid her altogether, because they were too uncomfortable to ask.

Perhaps my emphasis on team here sounds a bit clichéd, but I know – because I've been there – that in the world of business 'team' is very often glossed over. When you're on the 'dash for cash', it can easily become all about you. Sure, you say the right things and, in reality, work in a team anyway, but whenever the mind is allowed to drift, it drifts back to the self. But this is unsustainable, particularly if you want to get the best out of yourself – if you want to go from 'good to great'. In short, *you can't do this on your own.*

Assertive Humility

CHAPTER 5

Post cancer: hat free

Assertive Humility

I returned to work at Heinz in May of 2002, though it was a real struggle physically, emotionally and cognitively. My interest level in the job had been on the wane for some months before I left; now it was rock bottom.

On my thirty-third birthday, in the middle of June, I sat at my work computer watching the screensaver go around and around. Finally it hit me. What am I doing here? After the experience and challenge I had just been through, and with no guarantee that I would outlive my 'allotment' of two and a half years, here I was back in the same place I had started. What's more, given the spiritual shift I had been through, there was even less chance that I was ever going to enjoy this work again. It was like I had crossed that bridge over the river – made that 'first choice' decision – on some aspects of my life but not on one of the most critical: what I would do with myself.

In a conversation after a cancer support group that week, Peta and I discussed my situation. I shared with Peta that I was not coping and was at a loss. In that conversation we decided that I would take some time off work and give myself more time to heal: physically, emotionally, mentally and spiritually. After the upheaval and uncertainty of the last six months, there was no question in Peta's mind that this was the right decision and that we would be okay. How amazing to have such a supportive, selfless and loving wife! Her agreement was an act of realistic optimism, faith and courage, particularly in the context and memory of the loss of her own father. I look back on this conversation as one of the critical moments in my journey.

In a gesture for which I remain very grateful, the new CEO at Heinz told me to take off whatever time I needed to get well; we agreed on a year.

Later in the year I returned to Heinz to take part in a follow up to a workshop, run by Dr Sven Hansen of The Resilience Institute, that I had been involved in a year before. The topic had been, presciently, 'resilience'. I turned up wearing my bandana and, when Sven asked us to describe what we had implemented in the previous year, I proceeded to tell my story to him and the others in the room. Needless to say it was a bit more dramatic than everyone else's. Later Sven and I got chatting and he asked me what I was planning to do, to which I could give only a vague response. He said that I should join his organisation. It was obvious to him, given my business and consulting background, plus the journey I had been on. This was another key moment.

The decision to take up Sven's suggestion was both an easy choice and a difficult one. We would have a lot less financial security – initially none – as I would essentially be starting a new branch of the business from scratch. But it was also a real opportunity to take a more spiritual path and make a contribution. The pros outweighed the cons and in 2003 I started the Australian branch of The Resilience Institute. Now I was completely over that bridge and looking to a whole new future. For the first time in my life, I was pursuing a passion and a vocation rather than a career.

In June of 2004 we celebrated my thirty-fifth birthday in style. It was two and half years since my cancer diagnosis. I was not only still alive, having survived the prognosis provided reluctantly by my neurosurgeon, but scans showed no signs of any more malignant growth. I had shed my bandana (despite some people apparently thinking I was 'cool' for wearing it, not realising the circumstances) and was now hat free. For the first time ever, really, my life could not be easily defined by a single piece of headwear.

By the five-year mark my scan frequency had been reduced to every two years. We held another party, dubbed the 'Thank God You're Here' celebration. January 2012 marked a decade of clear scans since my diagnosis, so we held another party to commemorate that milestone.

I'm not really a party person, but each of these parties was as much a reason to thank, again, all those who had provided Peta and myself with never-ending support over the years as it was to enjoy myself. That said, the party-going Stuart Taylor of 2012 was a very different person from the Stuart Taylor of ten years earlier. The local constabulary who arrived to tell us to turn down the music agreed.

Since my diagnosis and bandana days it has been an amazing experience working with executives and staff in large corporations and government all over the globe, educators at all levels of our education system, survivors of natural disasters and prisoners in maximum-security prisons, helping all of them to improve resilience, performance and happiness. The common thread through each and every one of these diverse backgrounds, interactions and motivations is basic humanity: each individual's intention to improve their lives. The most amazing outcomes have been where that improvement goes beyond 'fixing one's sleep' or 'controlling one's emotions' to a real spiritual shift of consciousness. What a privilege it is to be a part of these journeys.

It is fair to say that the insights I am sharing in this book have been a product of what I have learned through my own spiritual journey, The Gawler Foundation, The Resilience Institute, further reading, research and academic study. However, it would be remiss of me to not acknowledge the learning I have had from the thousands of people I have worked with over the last decade as part of The Resilience Institute. This learning has come both via the direct wisdom of the participants of my workshops and via the debating, teaching, listening to and integrating of our concepts in numerous different contexts.

Evolving consciousness

In Chapter 2 I introduced the concept of 'stagnant consciousness', pointing out that having turned away from my Catholic upbringing and become absorbed by my engineering degree, I had 'mothballed my spiritual radar'. In the pages since then I have described how various obsessions and blocks combined to keep my consciousness stagnant at a low, egocentric level for many years. Yes, I became a loving husband and father, but beyond family my world was 'black and white'. I was obsessed with perfectionism, fairness and control. I was a master of the fabricated future and the stress that came with that, and I reinforced that stress by incessantly seeking the approval of others. I had maintained a strong sense of entitlement since my childhood.

If we revisit the earlier 'ego' diagram (seen again in Figure 7), it is clear that I had many of the bases covered. The emphasis did change over the years, as I switched from my Cub to Air Force to corporate hats, but the underlying egocentricity remained.

Consciousness and Personal Growth

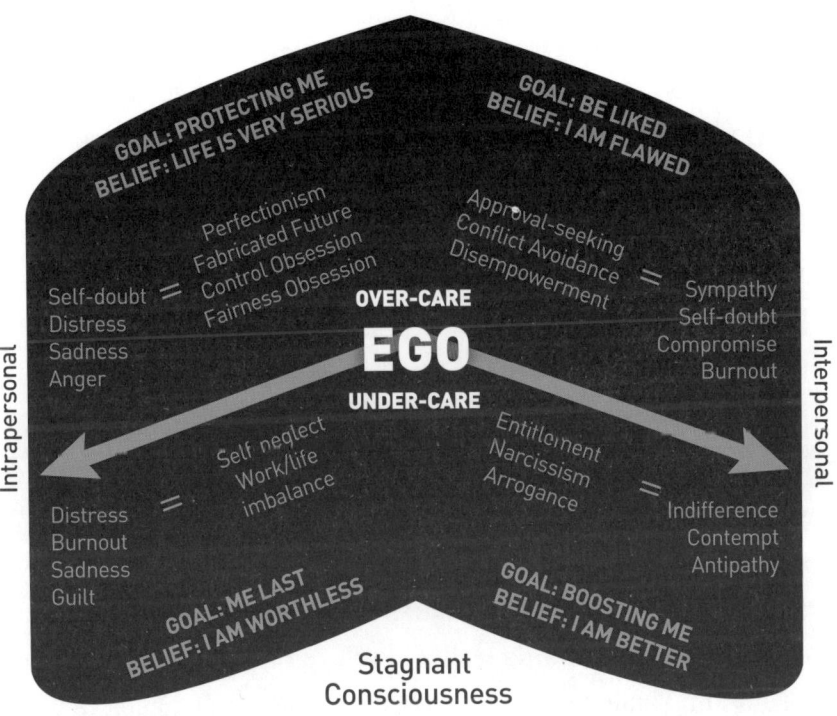

Figure 7: Forms of ego

In the last decade that has all changed. No longer stagnant, my consciousness has evolved, and continues to do so. My happiness today is much more authentic – not material based as in the past. I no longer feel 'entitled'; I am no longer obsessed by perfectionism, fairness and control. In fact, none of these makes sense to me anymore. I feel (and others, including Peta, agree) that I am a more rounded person than I was in the past. I am a vastly more spiritual person than I was; my sister recalls having 'tree hugging conversations' with me 'about meditation, spirit, the meaning of life', which would not have happened pre-cancer. Perhaps most importantly, I am a much more fulfilled person than I used to be. This is not to say that I have 'arrived' – not by any means – but I am much further ahead than where I started, and well on the way.

The important question, then – the question at the core of this book – is how has this substantial change come about, and how can others (perhaps including you) learn from my experiences and improve their own level of consciousness? How can someone who is stagnating, as I was, in an egocentric eddy of consciousness break free and move towards a more satisfying, more fully rounded level of consciousness – towards (as I will return to) 'assertive humility'? The solution, I believe, lies in accessing a number of 'enablers' that promote and support an ongoing evolution of consciousness.

Consciousness and Personal Growth

Figure 8: Enablers supporting evolution of consciousness

The first enabler: self-awareness

It all starts here: with self-awareness. For me, this came with a jolt via a cancer diagnosis. Having gone through what I went through in 2002, having had death in my immediate field of view for a couple of years, I had no choice but to start asking some bigger questions about life. A spotlight was directed at the life I had been living and it lit things up in a way that I had not expected. I started to question. I started to dissect the reasoning I had previously used to justify doing what I was doing, reacting as I was reacting, getting stressed as I had been getting stressed.

There is little doubt that meditation played a significant role for me in learning how to 'think about thinking' and come to terms with all I was going through. Prior to my cancer diagnosis, meditation was non-existent in my life. Had it approached me I would have waved it away, discounting it as the stuff of healing crystals and fluffiness. However, since being exposed to meditation while on the Gawler retreat, I have taken it on as a daily practice – something I continue to this day. Initially, meditation gave me a peacefulness, a sense of 'feeling good' that was very welcome while my world was being turned upside down. I was later able to apply meditation techniques to give me a greater sense of control while I was embedded in the medical system; it helped enormously during radiotherapy, my head held tight under that plastic mask.

My experience of meditation has led me to understand its ascribed benefits, including support for the immune system, energy, clarity, creativity, sleep, awareness, mindfulness, concentration, happiness and more[2].

While there would be other enablers and qualities that would push me towards a more evolved consciousness in the coming years (including some, such as positivity, which I was already unconsciously displaying), self-awareness was the critical first one. This was the enabler that cracked the shells of my obsessions.

If this book achieves nothing else, I hope it does foster a degree of self-awareness in you. What I have discovered is that self-awareness is an incredibly powerful starting place in the pursuit of fulfilment. And while my self-awareness largely revealed itself only after my cancer diagnosis, I don't believe that such a drastic interruption to your life is necessary in order to make some progress.

We can build self-awareness broadly in terms of body, emotions, thoughts and spirit:

- Awareness of my *body* comes when I am able to notice my energy levels have dropped or I have lost my calm. Neither of these was something I was attuned to while I wore my corporate hat, whereas today I am acutely aware of my energy levels most of the time. I recognise the importance of maintaining my energy, hence my efforts to install my gym

---

[2] There are many schools and philosophies teaching meditation. The priority is to find one that works at the basic level of building calm, awareness and mindfulness, as well as having the capacity to explore and enable the emergence of consciousness.

and meditation time in my 'garage' of time each day before anyone else gets a look in.

- Awareness of my *emotions* comes when I can detect negative and destructive emotions – when perfectionism or over-caring or ego have taken over. With my Cub hat on, these negative emotions flourished, as they have often at other stages of my life. Now I can identify these emotions as they bud, nip them before they flower and grow from the messages they were conveying.

- Awareness of my *thoughts* allows me to hear pessimistic chit-chat. I can identify when I am fabricating a worst-case scenario and allowing this fantasy to cause me stress. The stress of my early RAAF days at Amberley could have been reduced with more mindfulness of this type. These days I am much better able to check my thinking when stress arises and do a quick reality check on the source of that stress. The practice of meditation has been a hallmark of my progress here.

- Awareness of my spirit – my presence, compassion, values and purpose – builds as I am better placed to witness actions that deviate from my consciousness. This is something that was more or less foreign to me before my cancer diagnosis. Today I can catch myself responding automatically to a negative situation, such as in traffic, and consciously reassess my choices. Today I am much more attuned to what's going on around me, including the emotions and needs of others.

Now, if you are currently in a fast-paced management role or similar, you may be thinking I have lost touch with reality here. I hear you saying that it is very difficult to maintain perspective and awareness when you are operating at a million miles an hour. It is very hard to 'stop and smell the roses' when they are just a blur on the side of the road. I hear you suggesting that I have become a tree-hugging hippy. These are precisely the things I might have said myself a decade ago, before fate stepped in and forced me to see things differently.

Far from losing touch with reality, I would suggest I am now far more in touch with reality than I would have thought possible in the past.

I now recognise that the flat-out lifestyle is unsustainable in the long term – deep down, perhaps very deep down, you may recognise this yourself – and that if you want to avoid crashing and burning, then finding a way to gently apply the brakes is essential. Beyond that, slowing down can lead to more happiness and improved performance in all that you do.

The starting point is self-awareness.

The second enablers: rewiring beliefs and choices

Being aware of your reactions to situations is a start, but 'rewiring' your brain to fundamentally change your responses to those situations takes a shift in your beliefs. This shift begins with a transition from simple awareness to questioning, and potentially disputing, your automatic responses. (I won't revisit the earlier sections – in Chapters 2 and 4 – on beliefs and choices here, but hopefully having read those you now understand how central beliefs are to the way we choose to respond to situations.) It was through such shifts in belief that I was able to start moving beyond my various obsessions.

Take the fairness obsession, for instance. For most of my life when something 'unfair' happened I would react with anger or frustration, as many people do. So on getting stuck in traffic I would fume, curse, thump the steering wheel – the dysfunctional, 'do nothing' choice of Figure 6 on page 103. As my self-awareness started to grow, I started to reflect on that anger some time after the event that had prompted it. I then started to dispute the rationality of my reaction. Over time, as I described earlier, I was able to change my beliefs about this 'unfairness'. The choice I made in response to busy traffic changed from anger to acceptance.

Similarly with the perfectionist obsession and its partner, approval-seeking. When your goal is first and foremost to live, as mine was after my diagnosis, the need to be perfect becomes (when you're conscious of it) redundant. Of course I didn't shake this initially – the way I went about getting my organic diet in order bears testament to that – but I did become increasingly aware of it. Eventually I started catching myself in fabricated-future mode and questioning why, after all I had been through with my illness, I should be stressed about whether or not I might 'fail' in, say, the running of a workshop. The more my beliefs about my perfectionist obsession changed, the more relaxed I became about being imperfect.

A former neighbour of mine unknowingly brought home to me
one of the most powerful implications of self-awareness and
beliefs. He described how, for a number of years before my cancer
diagnosis, he would sometimes walk past our house while I was in
the front garden. When he did so, I would essentially ignore him.
He was a professional musician. He had long hair, a mean-looking
Staffordshire terrier, and people would come and go from his house
with guitars all the time. Whether or not that was the reason for my
failure to acknowledge him I don't know, but certainly at this time
I was self-absorbed (ego set to 'high') and not self-aware enough
to even consider that my lack of interest could be taken as rude or
even insulting.

Later, after my surgery, I grew to know this person through a friend.
He ended up teaching me some guitar and – something I would
never previously have imagined possible – gave me the confidence
to sing in public. These days he and I jam together at each other's
houses or at parties. The ability to play and sing has added an
enormous amount of fulfilment to my life.

This example demonstrates the strong tie between self-awareness
and beliefs. It was a change in my self-awareness that brought my
previous indifference to my new friend into sharp relief and led to
my allowing him into my life. That same self-awareness helped me
'see' myself when I got up to sing a song. I could witness my own
emotions and behaviours, ask myself how I felt, challenge myself to
move through any anxiety. In turn, that facilitated a change in my
beliefs about singing, from the belief that I would never be able to
sing well enough – read 'perfectly' – to justify singing in public, to

the belief that if I sang with passion and authenticity any technical shortfalls wouldn't matter and I would be able to connect with those who were listening.

This is probably a good time to recap where we've got to.

There is a wide range of behaviours – obsessions, dependencies and so on – associated with ego; each of those behaviours is underpinned by one or more beliefs about 'how the world is, or should be'. If these beliefs never change, they act as blocks to our consciousness, which remains stagnant. We keep making the same choices over and over; our focus remains egocentric.

With self-awareness, we can start to question and dispute these beliefs. If we embrace this questioning, we can start to actually change our beliefs, and then we can start making different choices. When that happens we are on the path to evolving consciousness. We start to move past ego and towards assertive humility.

That said, there are other enablers that play a role in a shift towards assertive humility, as were shown in Figure 8.

The third enablers: energy and calm

The role of energy as a block to the evolution of consciousness was described at some length in Chapter 3. I described how poor attention to my physical and mental energy levels – operating at full throttle for long periods of time – contributed to poor health. It also contributed to a closed mind: I simply didn't have the mental space to be thinking about anyone other than myself most of the time.

Post-cancer that changed as my beliefs around the importance of energy levels changed. As I described, my garage of time is now well stocked with time for myself – for exercise, meditation and so on – which paradoxically allows me a lot more room for others. In short, effective management of energy enables a move away from ego.

The ability to be calm has a similar effect. I have learnt a great deal about calmness – both achieving it and its benefits – from the regular practice of meditation. The effect, as I mentioned, is very powerful.

The fourth enablers: vulnerability and courage

Vulnerability and courage may at first glance seem to be opposites, but in practice the ability to act courageously has a lot to do with being comfortable with vulnerability. Brené Brown, author and thought leader on the topic of vulnerability and courage, defines vulnerability as facing uncertainty, risk and emotional exposure – a daring to show up and be ourselves. We can take a lead from sport here: watch the motorcycle racer or downhill skier, living life millimetres away from disaster. They are enormously courageous, but they can only show this courage by having come to terms with their intense vulnerability. The same link can be made between emotional courage and vulnerability. Which comes first? Well that depends.

Clearly in my case, adversity in the form of cancer was a catalyst for my shift in consciousness. That adversity brought vulnerability, whether I wanted it or not. For the period during and immediately after my illness I was highly vulnerable, both physically and emotionally. While, as I've discussed, Peta and I managed to maintain a level of realistic optimism, I was always just one visit to the doctor away from that optimism being shattered. During my surgery I was perhaps as vulnerable as it is possible to be, having someone play the *Operation* game on my actual brain.

I had little choice but to embrace this vulnerability, given its magnitude and the fact that I lived with it for a number of years. Ongoing health challenges mean that even today I live with a certain amount of vulnerability.

This is not a bad thing. Becoming comfortable with vulnerability has been essential to the evolution of my consciousness. It has allowed me to approach my 'post-cancer life' with the confidence to do everything from singing in public to establishing and running my own business. Some might even say I display a lot of courage in doing this, though in practice I have little choice (the choices other than positive action being untenable to me).

All of which begs the question: Is some form of vulnerability essential to 'switching on' one's consciousness? Clearly not everyone needs to get cancer in order to enjoy an evolved level of consciousness, but does a shift away from stagnant consciousness require that one's vulnerability be tested in some way?

The answer to these questions, I believe, is 'Yes'. But it need not be through adversity. There are other ways to show courage, other ways of becoming familiar with vulnerability, and they don't need to be at the earth-shattering level that my illness was for me. The important component is becoming comfortable with the vulnerability that comes with courage.

Take a typical business meeting scenario. Some years ago, on one of the large projects I worked on at KPMG, there was a KPMG audit partner who would regularly attend review meetings with me. After a few meetings, I noticed something about this person: she would never make the first comment when asked for an opinion. Rather, she would only ever offer an opinion after others had offered theirs, and when her opinion did come it would be a simple reinterpretation or rewording of what others had said. In other words, she never had the courage to offer up an original view on anything under discussion. This senior manager, who I knew by reputation was more than comfortable speaking out in the context of a boardroom – her comfort zone – felt vulnerable in the context of the project meetings because she did not know as much as others in the room. She was not willing to allow that vulnerability to show, as that would have threatened his ego.

This is a simple example of how courage – if shown – can be an enabler of evolving consciousness. Should this person have found the courage to offer up her own opinions, at the risk of being contradicted or corrected and potentially adjusting her view as a result, she would have started to move away from her egocentricity.

Another example might be the learning of a new skill – say a language. Anyone who has ever learnt a language, even just a few words for travel, will know that it is impossible to make real progress in the speaking of that language until you're ready to make mistakes. You have to be willing – have the courage – to join in on conversations and speak up in the knowledge that what you say may not be completely correct grammatically. You may even be laughed at occasionally for an inadvertent faux pas. This is exactly what a child does (without any concern for vulnerability) when learning his or her native language. Again, growth comes through comfort with vulnerability. In the words of my daughter (at around the age of five) to her older brothers when they were upset: 'You've got to learn to laugh at yourself!'

There is a clear distinction to be made here between theory and practice. In order to be effective as enablers, courage and vulnerability need to be embraced in the *doing* of them. To overcome the control obsession, for instance, you need to find and *experience* situations in life where you do not have control. Then during or after those experiences, you need to review them (self-awareness is obviously a prerequisite here), observe the emotion (shame, humour, embarrassment) and make peace with the vulnerability you felt.

The more you embrace vulnerability, the more courageous you will become as you face new challenges and adversity. This, as I will discuss further shortly, is a central component of assertive humility.

Compassion enablers: empathy and gratitude

At the end of the last chapter I described the role the 'team' played in helping me get through the early stages of my cancer, then the surgery, then my long recovery. Another enabler was at play here in the form of *gratitude*, or, more specifically, a willingness to be grateful. This was built on a recognition that I couldn't do it all myself (self-awareness again) and, therefore, a reaching out to others. Learning to be grateful also played a role in my adoption of another enabler: empathy.

Empathy lies at the centre of a model of social investment – the investment we make in our relationship with others and in response to the plights of others – I have built up over recent years. Since my cancer, Peta and I have been exposed to a wide variety of social responses. Compassion and 'social influence' have become a common thread in my spiritual exploration since diagnosis; I have tried to get a clearer view of the meaning of compassion and sought to apply it more in my own life. As I have clarified my thinking over the last few years with great input from and debate with Dr Sven Hansen at The Resilience Institute, I have positioned compassion relative to other forms of social investment, as in Figure 9. This perspective is important here because it investigates the interpersonal side of the ego, where most of our previous discussion, particularly around the obsessions, is much more intrapersonal (or self-focused).

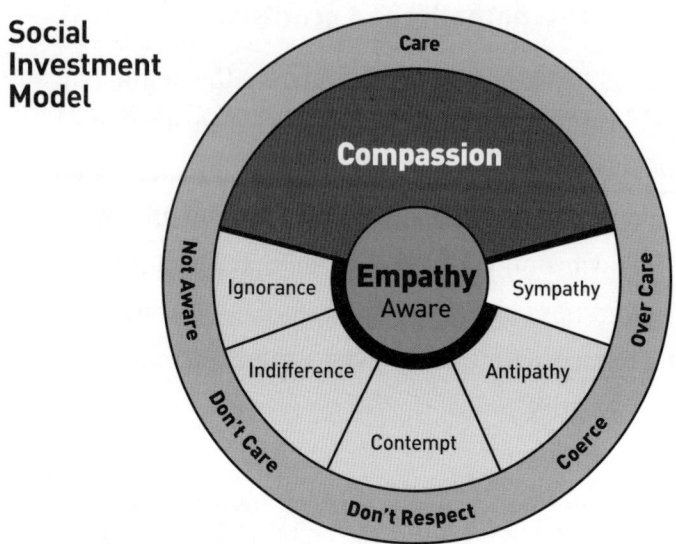

Social Investment Model

Figure 9: Social investment model

For a long time, feelings of compassion of any sort were completely foreign to me. Peta likes to recall how I would roll my eyes if she gave a donation to a tin-shaker. I had grown up on self-reliance and felt others should do the same. Combined with my high level of ego, my approach to social investment prior to my cancer had centred around ignorance, indifference and contempt (through entitlement). These responses weren't conscious – they were automatic, reptilian responses true to my ego-centredness.

The four grey-shaded responses in the social investment model – ignorance, indifference, contempt and antipathy – are all clearly ego-centred. The last three of these sit squarely in the 'under-caring' area of the main consciousness model I introduced earlier; I include ignorance here on the assumption that ignorance of another's situation can result from preoccupation with one's own beliefs, biases, assumptions, goals and time, and therefore a lack of space for those of others. This was certainly the case with me. Contempt is a passive choice of moral superiority that leads to disempowerment, disregard, disgust and dismissiveness. Interestingly, American psychologist Paul Ekman regards contempt as one of the fastest growing emotions in Western society. As dangerous, if not more so, is the active negative choice called antipathy, which I see as including bullying, prejudice, manipulation and political power play to meet my goals.

Perhaps counterintuitively, though I have already touched on this, 'sympathy' also sits in the ego-centred region of the model. When I am sympathetic, I feel sorry for others. I agree with and own the emotions and situation of the other person. At the same time, I am subconsciously focused on myself as strong and them as weak. I don't want conflict so don't call it as it is and/or aim for compromise, even if these are not in the best interests of the other person. As a result, I disempower the other person, which drains them (and me) emotionally over time.

My illness could easily have sent me down the path of sympathy. It is not uncommon for those who have suffered in some way to respond by showing unfiltered concern for the suffering of others. But not only is the 'soft love' of sympathy not in my nature, I didn't trust it. While my family had been exposed to a lot of genuine care following my father's death, many others had showered us with sympathy, seemingly wanting to 'save' us. I clearly remember it feeling more that these people wanted to feel good about themselves – to burnish their egos – than to show heartfelt care. This experience made me distrustful of sympathy, and even of compassion.

In my search to better understand compassion I have found that I have been more able to embrace it.

Buddhist teacher Sogyal Rinpoche describes compassion as: 'not a sense of sympathy or caring for the person suffering, not simply a warmth of heart toward the person before you, or a sharp clarity of recognition of their needs and pain, it is also a sustained and practical determination to do whatever is possible and necessary to alleviate their suffering. Compassion is not true compassion unless it is active'. A shorter definition might be: 'caring for and enabling self and others in pursuit of the greater good'.

Central to my acceptance of compassion as a desirable form of social investment has been an understanding of the distinction between sympathy and empathy, and in particular the notion that compassion can be supported by 'tough love'. Where previously I had rejected (inasmuch as I had thought about it at all) any form of compassion as an extension of sympathy, a more sophisticated understanding of empathy and compassion gave me permission to care while remaining assertive. I have been able to build on my firm and long-held views about the importance of self-responsibility while bridging those views with a willingness to see the other person's point of view and circumstances.

So there are many paths to a more open, or evolving, consciousness. Each of the enablers I have discussed in this section can play a part in shifting you out of stagnation, away from ego-centredness and towards assertive humility. However, none will get you very far on its own, and none will get you anywhere without the essential component of self-awareness plus, very importantly, a willingness to change.

The fundamental question here is this: Are you playing a part in the drama of your life, or are you simply a witness to the drama? Put another way, are you a passenger on the journey of your life, or are you the driver? (Hint: If you don't know, chances are it's the former.) Evolving consciousness is all about putting yourself into the driver's seat so that you can see what is going on around you and respond to it, consciously, in your own way.

It has been interesting for me to realise, with hindsight, that the seeds of my own evolving consciousness were sown at KPMG via the coaching I received from my mentor, my KPMG partner and others. Their honest feedback about, say, my facilitation efforts, was instrumental in the development of my ability to reflect on my own performance, to start letting go of the control obsession and to become comfortable with a level of vulnerability. I was able to embrace the enablers of courage and vulnerability with some success because the competence and compassion of these colleagues, who had only my interest at heart, helped me appraise my work without excessively reverting to my other obsessions of perfectionism and approval-seeking. (As an aside, this is where building your own awareness through the feedback of others is something that should be done with caution, for it relies on those others having little in the way of their own ego, being compassionate and genuinely caring about you. There are many who are only too willing to give advice; there are few who are able to do so with genuine authenticity.)

However, while the access I gained to certain enablers from people like my partner and my mentor at KPMG was worthwhile, it was necessarily limited to work, and within that to the specific circumstances around project management and facilitation. My consciousness during this period was still stagnant. The seeds may have been sown but they weren't germinating just yet, predominantly because they were still lacking the fertiliser of self-awareness.

As we have seen, the real starting point of my journey of awakened consciousness was the cancer retreat in which those of us participating spent a good amount of time in reflection on the past. This helped me to see my whole life to that point with a new set of glasses. It gave me the ability to look back at some event or time in my life and say to myself, 'Well, I could have done that better'. Meditation gave me the ability to be calm. Practice at reassessing yourself from a distance like that leads to the ability to do the same thing from a closer perspective, to look back on your day, for instance, and reflect on 'what worked and what didn't' in terms of your personal responses to the situations that confronted you. If you were stressed, where was the stress coming from? Was it, in retrospect, driven by some form of fabricated future? If you made decisions, how much were those decisions driven by ego – by your own concerns rather than those of others?

One way to think about this sort of reflection is as the collection of data points. Each time you are able to look back at a situation and think about your response to it – an instance of stress or anger, a choice, a battle for control, etc. – represents one data point. As you build a (mental) database of these points, your analysis will come more easily. And it will require less 'distance', to the point where – and this is the ultimate aim – you are able to 'witness' your response to a situation as it happens.

It is at this point – when you can witness yourself taking action or thinking a thought as you are doing so – that all the enablers of evolving consciousness start to become available to you. You are now, as I put it above, witnessing the drama of your life rather than merely playing a part in it. Now you are able to make choices about the way you respond to circumstances in real time, and that means you are more likely to make more reasoned, sensible choices – choices that help master stress and maximise the welfare of yourself and those around you. You can make conscious choices about energy management, about social investment (empathy vs sympathy vs compassion, for instance), about allowing yourself to be courageous and vulnerable. As this happens, you are starting to gain a measure of control over your own life, not in a way that makes life predictable, but in a way that makes your responses to whatever life throws at you more of your own choosing. You can then explore the next challenge.

This brings us full circle, back to the concept of 'flow' that I raised in the early discussion about perfectionism and the pressure-performance curve. Recall that 'flow' is a state of full engagement in the present, in which ego is set aside and consciousness is high. Flow is essential to achieving a fulfilled, authentically happy life. None of this is to say that an evolving consciousness needs necessarily to lead to major changes to your life. What it does do is provide you with more freedom to make choices. To paraphrase the author of *Flow*, Mihaly Csikszentmihalyi, we need to become independent of the social environment and 'no longer respond exclusively in terms of its rewards and punishments'. We must 'develop the ability to find enjoyment and purpose regardless of individual circumstances'.

In other words, an evolving consciousness – brimming with self-awareness, energy, gratitude, empathy, challenges, learning and so on – can make us happier and can help us re-engage our spirit with the world around us. That helps us be a better person for those around us – whether or not it leads to change in any other circumstances of our life. As our consciousness continues to evolve, we approach the very powerful state of assertive humility.

CHAPTER 5 – Post cancer: hat free

Assertive Humility

CHAPTER 6

Assertive Humility

Assertive Humility

As my journey continues – as my consciousness keeps on evolving – I believe I am now approaching something I call 'assertive humility'. This needs some exploration.

Assertive humility is not humility, and it's not assertiveness either. Each has value on its own, but together they represent something much more. Together they represent a natural positive tension.

Humility on its own can be perceived in Western society as being meek and mild, exhibiting false modesty or even subordination. But this seriously misinterprets the true meaning and weight of the word.

A better way to think about humility is as an antonym of ego, what Sogyal Rinpoche calls 'egolessness'. Some describe it simply as cherishing others over self. I subscribe to Buddhist monk Matthieu Ricard's interpretation when he says that in a state of true humility one's self image no longer needs protection. At this point, all the obsessions, dependencies, self-neglect and detachment associated with ego have been left behind. Now, the truly humble person is able to make value-based decisions, without regard for him or her self. Decisions are based on the greater good, rather than self-protection or self-enhancement. It should go without saying that achieving this to a high degree requires a highly evolved level of consciousness. However, increasing one's humility is certainly within the power of any self-aware individual.

Humility is often considered one of the key attributes of modern leadership. Jim Collins, in his work *Good to Great*, studied Fortune 500 companies and their CEOs to determine which companies succeeded over an enduring period and why. His concept of a highest order 'Level 5 leader' is underpinned by two attributes: humility and a drive to succeed. In coining the term 'assertive humility', I don't seek to supplant Collin's second attribute of 'drive', which he defines as being 'infected with an incurable need to produce results'. Whilst 'drive' can be applied to good and 'evil' (or misguided) goals – witness recent corporate, sporting and religious collapses – assertiveness in contrast is a spiritual concept based on adherence to a strong sense of values.

Assertiveness is also a sometimes blurred and misunderstood term. It is occasionally confused with aggressiveness and even physical or psychological abuse, though it is neither of these. As mentioned, it is steadfast adherence to a strong set of values. It involves the intention and practice of acting on those values while maintaining empathy and compassion for others. Assertiveness can be used in a debate or discussion with anyone from a work colleague or superior to a family member, or in any situation in which your rights, or those of someone else, need standing up for. It can be enacted by being the first to voice an opinion on a controversial or complex topic, particularly when that opinion is at odds with a general consensus view. Again, courage is a prerequisite.

We end up with more than a sum of the parts when these two words are combined. To restate what I wrote in the prologue of this book, assertive humility means having more care and compassion for both others and myself while my behaviour, decisions and expressed opinions are consistent with my values and beliefs. Assertive humility is an approach to life that is characterised by equanimity, not superiority or inferiority, and by presence with, not distance from, others. It comes with a sense of purpose and a sense of modesty. It is, simply, a more authentic way to be for both yourself and those around you.

Put another way, assertive humility is where you get to when you have mastery of all the enablers we have been discussing – when you draw on those enablers at all times without conscious awareness that you are doing so. The qualities of assertive humility emerge from these enablers. They are summarised along the top line of the consciousness model we have been discussing, shown again in Figure 10. They can, like ego, be divided into both the intrapersonal and the interpersonal, with compassion – for both self and others – sitting in the centre.

An important note before I go on, though. While I write at times as though assertive humility is a destination, it is more fluid than that. There is always room to grow, always room for even more assertive humility as your consciousness continues to evolve. It might be better to think of the enablers and qualities of assertive humility acting in a circular and lifting manner: the enablers reveal the qualities, which strengthen access to the enablers further, which enrich the qualities further, and so on. So, as we start to discuss the qualities of assertive humility, don't think of them as 'either/ors' but rather as levels of development.

Consciousness and Personal Growth

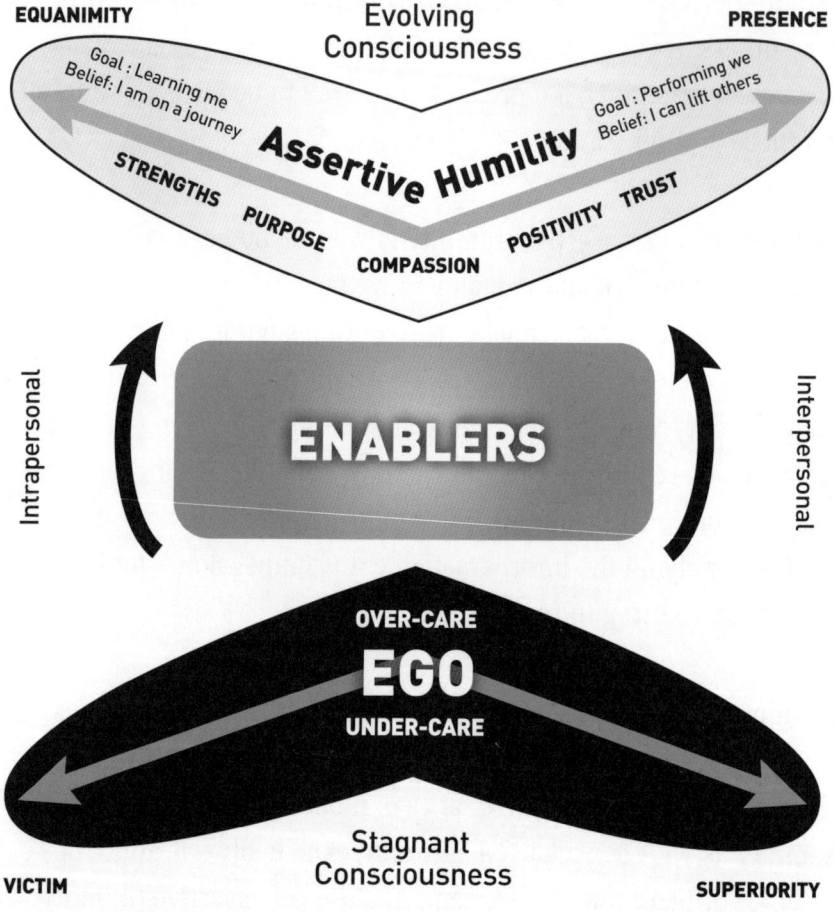

Figure 10: Elements of assertive humility

On the intrapersonal side is *purpose*. We might equally call this 'direction'. It is a sense of clarity about where one is heading, or 'what I'm here for'. It need not be explicitly named, but it needs to be very clear to you. For instance, I gained a strong sense of purpose when I made the decision to cross the bridge of my drawing – not to revert to my 'old' life – after recovering from my cancer. This sort of robust sense of purpose, perhaps more a feeling than anything concrete, is an essential quality of assertive humility. Purpose provides a reliable yardstick for measuring and using assertiveness: 'I know what is important, how it contributes and how strongly I will pursue it.'

By the nature of the term assertive humility, the 'purpose' quality being discussed here isn't just any purpose, but rather a purpose positioned for the 'greater good'. In other words, it represents a higher-order intention to improve the world or a situation beyond self. This is clearly a humble perspective. Hence, it is purpose that provides the spiritual platform for assertive humility and it is purpose that provides a compass for the other qualities.

For some time after my diagnosis I had a crisis of purpose. Unless I was able to achieve clearer direction, my recovery was going to be hampered. Starting to work in the space of helping others to reach their potential eventually provided that purpose. What's more, it was a purpose that for the first time in my life that was about the 'greater good'. Of course, my purpose will continue to evolve.

Strengths needs some explanation.

Most of us – probably all of us – have things we do really well. Things for which, while we are doing them, time seems to stop.

Assertive Humility

We are at one with the task, completely engaged in it and all but oblivious to external distraction. This might only happen for moments at a time, or for hours. It might happen at home (playing music, solving a cryptic crossword, exercising) or at work (running a meeting, interviewing job candidates, 'big picture' planning).

This is what sportspeople refer to as being 'in the zone', when all the stars align and they are able to perform at their very best, with all-encompassing focus and no self-doubt. It is the athlete who competes (in his mind) with no one but himself and produces a personal best. It is the concert pianist who produces an exquisite performance and melts the audience in the process. It is the sculptor who carves a masterpiece from a piece of stone without consciously thinking about what she is doing.

It is also what Csikszentmihalyi is referring to when he describes the state of 'flow'. When you are working in an area of strength, the intensity of the work becomes almost irrelevant: hard work just engages you more deeply. You operate right at the top of that pressure-performance curve. Csikszentmihalyi makes the point that flow is 'characterised by positive emotions and a total loss of ego'. This loss of ego is the important point about operating in a state of strength in this way. It means being the best you can be, but only for yourself – with no concern, again, about self-image.

Operating in an area of strength provides a solid platform for further development of assertive humility. It provides us with the 'luxury' of not having to question our own abilities and adequacies; it provides the opportunity to thrive effortlessly and naturally. In so doing it gives us more freedom to focus on the needs of others.

The clear prerequisite here, with respect to approaching assertive humility, is purpose – purpose positioned for the greater good as described above. Without purpose, it is completely possible to achieve flow by operating in an area of strength. But doing so does not lead you closer to assertive humility. For instance, when I was at KPMG I loved facilitating workshops and driving change. This was a time when I spent a lot of my day in flow because by this stage facilitation had become a real strength. But none of this was about the greater good; I was certainly not operating with assertive humility. I was more interested in the accolades of others – in receiving recognition that I had done an amazing job. In contrast, when I work with a group in a workshop today, I am usually operating in flow *with purpose*. My reward comes from seeing the growth in my participants, not myself.

When our strengths are put into action via our spiritual purpose, we reach the peak quality of assertive humility on the intrapersonal side: *equanimity*. Equanimity is complete comfort in oneself – in 'your own skin'. It's a place of recognition that you are neither superior nor inferior to anyone else. It's not, importantly, a state of perfection, where all in life is rosy. Rather, it's a state of surety in the knowledge that life will go on no matter what failures, misfortunes or setbacks you face. It's a confidence that, at a deep level, you are a worthy person who will prevail.

Trepidation and anxiety were common during the periods of my first three hats. When these threaten today, my personal dialogue around equanimity first and foremost recognises the fabricated-future nature of the stress; understands that the associated forecast is imaginary; shores up confidence from previous experience; accepts the possibility that should things come unstuck there will also be a learning opportunity; and refocuses on the present task at hand as aligned to my strengths and the 'greater good' purpose beyond self and ego.

As with all the qualities of assertive humility, equanimity is both the end and the start. To reach a state of equanimity is to understand that you still have a long way to go – that no matter how much you learn, how much your consciousness evolves, there will always be more evolution to come. Perhaps paradoxically, coming to this understanding of 'eternal incompleteness' provides a significant contribution towards a deep and authentic happiness.

On the interpersonal side of assertive humility, the first quality we find is *positivity*. As with vulnerability, we have already discussed this in some detail in Chapter 3, so I will limit the coverage here. In that chapter I addressed positivity largely from a personal perspective. Similar principles, measures and benefits also arise when the concept is applied interpersonally. Suffice to say that a functionally positive attitude in the approach you take to those around you is a fundamental aspect of assertive humility. Being positive – just as my KPMG mentor was after our client's near meltdown – lifts those around you. Positivity engages others; it is a prerequisite for influence. At a primitive level it signals inclusiveness and acceptance rather than opposition or threat. It lifts the consciousness of all, improving overall clarity not just at a task level but also in terms of purpose. The challenge is to generate positivity in self and others in an authentic way based on creating a vision of a hopeful future, having contentment in and gratitude for the present, and celebrating the past.

That *trust* is a quality of assertive humility seems obvious in some ways, but it is not as straightforward as it may seem. Personally, trust has always been very important to me – it's something I see as a core value. But I have learnt that the aspiration to be trustworthy is one thing. Actually achieving trust, in the eyes of others, can be something else, particular when ego gets in the way. So in my days as a junior officer in the Air Force, for instance, I sincerely wanted my team to trust me, but if I made a mistake, was I willing to admit it? Not always, because while a desire for trust was pulling me in one direction, protection of self-image (perfectionism, over-caring – not wanting to appear vulnerable) was pulling me in the other. In those days the latter would tend to win out, meaning I might maintain my self-image (by not admitting a mistake) while at the same time undermining trust within my group. Of course, I was unaware of the complexities of all this at the time.

My exploration and understanding of trust started many years ago when a wise person said to me, 'If you want to build trust it is quite simple: do what you say you will do – again and again and again. Over time, your track record builds and so does trust.' This process is far more challenging if you have breached trust in the first place. Beyond this basic tenet there are many other elements that will create or destroy trust. Are my decisions rooted in consistent values? Do I tell the truth? Do I provide maximum transparency of information? Do I use power with respect? Do I create a culture of candour? Do I treat contrarians with compassion? Are my goals centred on the greater good? Do I resolve conflict with dignity? Do I admit my mistakes? Have I taken the time to understand the people around me at a personal level?

As my consciousness has evolved and I have moved away from ego-centredness, I feel I have been better able to match my desire to build trusting relationships with the ability to actually do so. This is a good example of how the characteristics of assertive humility necessarily work together. Being trusted by people you lead is essential to the goal of liberating their best performance, but being genuinely trustworthy requires comfort in vulnerability at a minimum, and preferably a high degree of equanimity. Trust operates on a number of levels, from the desire to be trusted (as in my junior officer period) at one end of the scale, to complete and genuine trust – even through adversity and change at the other. The higher your equanimity, the greater chance you have of achieving a high level of trust.

The interpersonal equivalent of equanimity is *presence*. When equanimity is combined with strong compassion for self and others, we have the opportunity to reach out to others with presence – the ultimate expression of assertive humility. Put another way, I define presence simply as 'assertive humility personified'. It is the observable, behavioural manifestation of living the principles of assertive humility.

Presence should not be confused with arrogance. Arrogance is rooted either in a delusional self-assessment of one's talents relative to a given challenge, or as an attempt to shore up a known inadequacy by 'going on the offensive'. Or, as discussed earlier in Chapter 3, arrogance can stem from the under-caring positions of detachment, aloofness and entitlement. Over time, people operating from this space breed contempt (two-way), destroy trust and quash empowerment, learning and creativity in others.

There is no shortage of famous people we could nominate as having a high level of presence: Nelson Mandela, the Dalai Lama and Barack Obama are fairly obvious examples. It would be easy to believe that they were born this way. However, observing the 'fall' that occurs when someone previously regarded as high in presence behaves in an inauthentic way (think any of the infamous drug cheats in elite sport) illustrates the behavioural and spiritual components of presence. When others observe someone with presence they witness someone operating true to their values, high in equanimity and not afraid to speak their position, and with strong empathy and compassion for others.

So which people stand out as great examples of assertive humility? No doubt we can name many from history, such as Mother Theresa, Nelson Mandela (again!) and Gandhi. Equally there will be countless unknown people who also live in accordance with this concept. I chose people to write the forewords and testimonials for this book based on my observations of them as examples of assertive humility. Dr Charlie Teo is a highly respected neurosurgeon who also drives the Cure for Life Foundation, seeking a cure for brain cancer in the next 10 years by integrating world medical resources to this single task. Rebecca McGrath sits on the boards of many global corporations, leads with strength and care, and mentors many women to make a contribution in the business world. Dr Ian Gawler was diagnosed with cancer in 1975 and went on to create The Gawler Foundation to help hundreds of thousands of cancer and MS patients to take positive action or make peace with respect to their situation. Dr Sven Hansen discovered through his executive medical experience that the corporate world was crying out for a positive and integral approach to succeeding in business and established The Resilience Institute to provide that wisdom and coaching (to over 30,000 people at the last count). Bob Santamaria leads the global legal team of a multinational bank – a complex, high-pressure role if ever there was one. Yet to see him work is to see equanimity at its strongest: calm, composure and inclusiveness personified. Last, but certainly not least, Dean Salter is a senior leader in BP. In working with Dean over a number of years it was clear that he is a strong leader with deep, authentic care for his people. In 2012, Dean was diagnosed with cancer. I have been amazed at the dignity, openness, humility and fight that he has shown through this process. Without question, Dean is experiencing his own emergence.

If this all makes assertive humility seem hard, even unattainable, it should. It's hard enough just to find compassion, or a sense of purpose, or to engage positively with the world, let alone to combine all of these and more. But in aspiring to assertive humility we are aspiring to a highly evolved level of consciousness, sitting many storeys above the ground floor of ego and stagnant consciousness, and in a building with no elevators, just stairs. However, while I wouldn't claim to have reached the high levels yet, I can say that the climb is worth it, and the view gets better and better the higher I go. Further, in a circular sort of way, the possession of the spirit needed to start that climb, not knowing how long it's going to take, indicates the potential to succeed.

Spirit for good

As I was preparing to go to the cancer retreat shortly after my diagnosis in 2002, Peta suggested that I use the retreat to explore my spirituality. I turned to her and said, 'I'm not sure I know what that word means'. I had been born into a Catholic family and, as I described early in this book, had been a committed churchgoer in my childhood. When I turned away from religion as an engineering student, I also turned away from spirituality. To me they were one and the same – spirituality without religion was not something I contemplated then, nor over the ensuing years.

Cancer, Ian Gawler and the following decade changed all that. I did, as Peta had suggested, start exploring the notion of spirituality while on the cancer retreat. I explored it in more depth during my subsequent year off work, and have continued to do so ever since.

Would I – could I – have discovered the spiritual side of myself without getting sick, confronting death and taking a full year out to think? I'd like to think that I would have eventually. Many do as they get older, but at the same time many don't until it's so late in their career, their marriage and the lives of their children that it has little impact. Certainly, as we have seen, my level of self-awareness was low all round prior to my illness: my spirituality was showing little or no sign of emerging.

'Why should it have?', you may ask. I was flying along nicely with my corporate hat on. I was playing a lead role in significant reorganisations involving the closure of factories and head savings in the thousands. There was no place for a 'soft and fuzzy' spiritual side – it would have distracted from the hard-edged world of balancing budgets and getting things done. And while I was losing interest in the Heinz role before my diagnosis, I would eventually have found myself a role in the mergers and acquisitions team in some other high-powered firm, or something similar, and continued on my way, pedalling hard and earning a healthy salary.

The answer to that question, I have since understood, is that the lack of spirituality in my life was blinding me to life's harsh realities. When it came to factory closures, for instance, I was not seeing the connection between a job loss and the impact that would have on numerous other people (spouses, children, local businesses, etc.). Whether or not my decisions were the right ones for the firm, I was not even *conscious* of their impact.

In a similar way, lack of spiritual awareness across organisations continues to cause widespread disharmony between individuals and teams. People jump to conclusions, make assumptions, and label others ('Those people in finance always say "no"!'). Workplaces are awash with indifference about and contempt for others – not necessarily those working close by but unseen or distant individuals who are more readily seen as a 'just a number'. This is why incorporating the spirit is important, even in the most hard-nosed of business situations.

What I now understand is that tapping into our spiritual nature through authentic behaviour is central to building sustainable performance in ourselves, our communities and our organisations. The exploration and enactment of our spiritual nature allows us to keep challenges and adversities in perspective, maintain a sense of humour and comfort in vulnerability, and make healthier choices. It leads to greater compassion, in which the starting point is one of care and empathy, which leads in turn to greater respect and trust, to a feeling of having made a real contribution, to flow, authentic happiness and assertive humility.

This is not about working any less hard, nor forgetting the bottom line. It is about building people (including yourself) and organisations that will thrive in the long term, no matter what is thrown at them.

If I sound in any way evangelical about this it is because I can look back and see the enormous canyon I crossed as a result of contracting cancer. Learning about self-awareness, consciousness and spirit has been a journey of 'Wow! I didn't even know this stuff was out there'. And I am very aware that that remains the case for a large number of people who work hard and fast, and who never slow down enough to even think that there might be a more conscious way of living – a way of living that will allow them to become better people while still, if they choose, pursuing the career path they are on.

For me it is different. I realised after a time that my old definition
of success, which was mostly about title and material success, was
ultimately making me sick. I'll never know whether my approach
to life contributed to my cancer, but I do know that it was eating
away at my energy levels and physical and emotional health. I
realised that I had to change and be a 'better' person, which for me
meant taking on challenges that I found meaningful, as opposed to
challenges that had no real purpose other than, say, to put money
into the pockets of faceless shareholders.

My new definition of success continues to evolve. I try to maintain
the more productive elements of my previous hats: the childish
nature of the Cub hat; the loyalty to team of the RAAF hat; the
drive and determination of the corporate cap; and, above all, the
vulnerable, inquisitive, exploring and compassionate attributes
of the bandana. For the time being I'm not wearing any particular
hat. I keep myself open to the possibility of future challenges,
opportunities and contributions, whatever they may be. I hope my
consciousness will continue to be awakened.

I hope that this book might have awakened *your* spiritual
consciousness.

Consciousness and Personal Growth

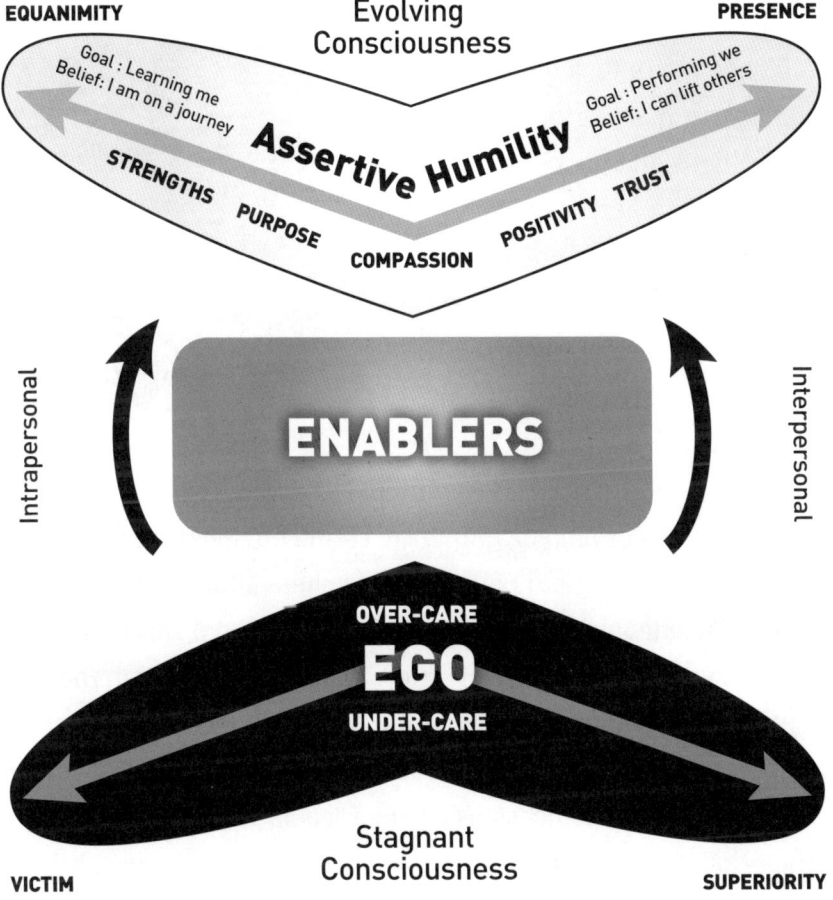

About the Author

Stuart Taylor is a director and board member of The Resilience Institute, a global organisation that works with organisations and people to liberate human performance sustainably. Closer to home, Stuart also leads The Resilience Institute in Australia. He is an experienced management consultant with a focus on resilience, performance and cognition. His diversity of qualifications in psychology, finance, IT and engineering bring a breadth of credibility and perspective to client situations. Stuart has worked extensively in government, professional services, the banking and finance sector, telecommunications and in the manufacturing sector. Prior to joining The Resilience Institute, Stuart was an associate director with KPMG Management Consulting and then worked as a senior leader in a global corporation. Stuart's clients include GE, BP, Jetstar Airways, KPMG, PwC, NAB, Citigroup, the Australian Government, CBA, Australia Post, Heinz and Port Phillip Prison.

Stuart Taylor is an energetic, empathic and motivational speaker with an ability to quickly connect with his audience at an emotional level. He is often complimented for authentically sharing his own personal resilience journey in recovering from cancer.

In 2002, while climbing the ladder to corporate executive, Stuart was diagnosed with brain cancer: prognosis 2.5 years. Far from accept the prognosis, Stuart embarked on a journey back to physical, emotional, cognitive and spiritual health. Part of this journey included creating The Resilience Institute in Australia to share his experience and philosophy with Australian organisations. Stuart's road to full recovery has been one of enormous personal growth and he is going from strength to strength.

About The Resilience Institute

The Resilience Institute is a global organisation that works with organisations and people to liberate human performance sustainably. Based in Australia, New Zealand, Singapore, China and Europe, The Resilience Institute works with senior executives and the entire employee base to build organisational and personal resilience.

Resilience is "...ultimate competitive advantage in the age of turbulence – when organisations are being challenged to change more profoundly, and more rapidly, than ever before." (leading strategist Gary Hamel, *Harvard Business Review*)

The Resilience Institute uses an evidence-based approach to introduce the personal disciplines of sustainable high performance within a meaningful life. The Resilience Institute achieves sustainable and measurable improvements using assessment instruments, consulting reviews, workshop interventions and personal coaching.

For further information about The Resilience Institute, visit www.resiliencei.com

About Cure For Life Foundation

Our Mission

Drive greater investment to accelerate brain cancer research into the cause, mechanism, treatment and prevention in Australia.

Our Vision

To accelerate a cure for brain cancer.

About the Cure For Life Foundation

Cure For Life Foundation is the largest fundraiser for brain tumour research and awareness in Australia. Established in 2001 by world-renowned neurosurgeon Dr Charlie Teo, Cure For Life Foundation is making a major contribution to the research of brain cancer.

Values of the Cure For Life Foundation

Excellence
Innovation
Ethical Responsibility

The Crane

An origami crane was chosen as the symbol for the Foundation because in Japanese legend it represents longevity and good fortune. With your help, the Foundation can help make these things possible for people suffering from brain tumours.

Message from Dr Charlie Teo

"People continue to believe that cancer is a disease that strikes as you get older. I saw 23 patients last week. Twenty were diagnosed with malignant brain cancer. Eight of those diagnosed were under 16 years old. We need to change the statistics on brain cancer survivorship. We need significant funds injected now into research to reduce brain cancer related deaths."

"There is no known cure for brain cancer, yet it has the greatest impact on society of all the cancers."

A donation of 10 per cent of all profits from sales of *Assertive Humility* will be made to Cure For Life Foundation

Cure For Life Foundation™

Accelerating treatments for brain cancer

What others are saying about *Assertive Humility*

"The power of the authentic voice. We know when someone is speaking from the profound insight offered by major personal trauma and change. We know that is a voice worth listening to.

Stuart Taylor was living the corporate dream – until cancer fractured it all. A poor prognosis; challenging, difficult treatment options; the family plunged into chaos. But amidst it all, the questions surfaced: What does it mean? How do I re-invent my life? How can others benefit from my experience? What can be learnt from all of this?

Plenty really. Stuart comments: "Barring a life-threatening illness, what does it take to force a crazy-busy, work absorbed person to question the wisdom of what they are doing?"

The delight of someone who has been through all this and survives to speak authentically is that there is no judgement. Just a well-crafted analysis of how easy it is to become immersed in the allure and busyness of day-to-day life, to live under the weight of stress and to fall into accepting the unacceptable as the norm.

Then we share the privilege of Stuart's new life; his new way of seeing things. The introspection, the insights and the re-prioritisation. For this is not about working less hard or forgetting the bottom line. This is about a new focus, a new paradigm.

Assertive Humility is about a new way of doing business that is gaining momentum in small offices and big boardrooms around the world. How to work with ethical purpose and personally satisfying meaning. How to take joy and humour and compassion into the workplace, to flourish, to be resilient, to foster respect and trust.

Perhaps all this sounds like a dream? But Stuart's life, both in his transition and in how he works now, is a fine example of how this dream really is attainable.

The secret? It is about supporting people and building organisations in a way that fosters authentic behaviour and assertive humility.

Assertive humility. What a great juxtaposition of two seminal words. How to do it? Well, that is what the book is all about!

This is a book to read, to savour, to contemplate and to put into action. When you do, going to work will become even more of a joy, and coming home a satisfying delight! Read it yourself, share it with your colleagues. They will thank you for it."

Dr Ian Gawler, OAM, Founder – Gawler Foundation; author of *Meditation: An In-Depth Guide* and *The Mind that Changes Everything*

"Stuart Taylor has confronted leadership challenges from early in his career but no-one should have to face a malignant brain cancer at 33 with a young family. Stuart's story is forged in this brutal reality and is an epic of courage and resilience. Having travelled with Stuart as a colleague for nearly 15 years he has been an inspiration for our work in leadership and resilience. The transformation in Stuart, his family, community and his work can only be described as heroic.

Sometimes we need to be rudely awakened. My hope is that readers might be gently brought to their senses by this book. My own mentor reminded me that "life is a conspiracy to put us to sleep". In today's brutally fragmented and high velocity world of work it is very easy to fall asleep. Stuart's story is a call to wake up and discover the deep and meaningful reality that sits quietly waiting in each of us. This is the real work of our lives and our leadership."

Dr Sven Hansen, Founder, Global CEO and Chairperson – The Resilience Institute

---

"I have had the pleasure of working with Stuart and his team from The Resilience Institute to build both leadership and sustainability capabilities into my team, which is spread over more than thirty countries.

Stuart's journey is such a great example of both resilience and humility – not just in the face of work difficulties but in the face of personal survival. Difficulties which left him perfectly placed to guide those facing their own personal challenges.

I have learnt over many years that the mark of many great leaders is humble exercising of positive influence. Leaders (and others, but especially leaders) need to be a source of positive energy – not fake cheerfulness. Leaders need to be positive especially when they themselves are feeling down. I talk to my leadership team about the privilege and burdens of leadership which I find to be more part of the experience of leadership than any glory! This all requires resilience and humility.

Through the lens of Stuart's story, reflections and learnings, this book brings these concepts to life and represents a powerful way of reminding oneself of the importance of the need for quiet reflection on such concepts.

I highly recommend this book to anyone who is either struggling with challenges in life, either professional or personal or who simply is open to a better way of living one's life."

Bob Santamaria, Chief Counsel ANZ Banking Corporation

"Stuart Taylor's story provides great insights with extraordinary humility and a deeply important reminder that we don't have to be passengers when it comes to chronic illness – there is much we can do to help ourselves. *Assertive Humility* is a source of inspiration as well as great learning for me.

Furthermore, for those who don't have a chronic illness, it's an incredibly valuable 'heads up' on what may signal an unsustainable lifestyle, and a personal guide on how to intervene and head things off at the pass should you find yourself in that situation. For me it reinforces my view that what I can do for myself in my cancer journey is ultimately more important than what medicine can do for me. That's not to in any way discredit the medical fraternity and the contribution they make to the healing process – they clearly have an important role to play – but learning how to live sustainably (which is essentially what this book is about) is very much within our control and will ultimately play the most significant role in healing.

Taylor's analysis of perfectionism, approval and judgement, control and ego (particularly the piece on under-caring and over-caring) really got my attention. I found myself looking in the mirror. And that's comforting in many ways; understanding what got me to the point of a chronic illness must be the access point to sustainable healing.

What I've found so far is that as I've become more aware of the dysfunction in my life that lead to my illness, there's a tension that emerges. On the one hand, I'm comforted by the growing awareness; on the other, having identified some of the problems, there's a natural sense of urgency to find and implement solutions. I guess it's the way I've operated right throughout my corporate life. Yet, in this situation, what to do isn't quite so straightforward and the patience required getting to the answers and the commitment required to implement the changes requires a lot more conviction than any other change I've made. So when I got to the chapter on 'enablers' (and Taylor's experience in implementing them) I felt very encouraged and inspired. It makes it all so possible and real.

As I continue on this journey, I'm increasingly recognising that it's full of immense opportunity and possibility. It's forcing me to make changes that are slowly transforming me as a person – I think I'm becoming a much better person as a result. Stuart's book is a gift within that context; it's another 'green shoot' of growth for me – many thanks for sharing it Stuart."

Dean Salter, Senior Executive, BP Australia